SCOTTISH BOOKPLATES

Brian North Lee
&
Ilay Campbell

U

Please note
It m

Fi

FIDE · ET · FIDUCIA

Sʳ James Primerose of Carington Barronet

Rᵒ Wood sculp

SCOTTISH BOOKPLATES

Brian North Lee
&
Ilay Campbell

The Bookplate Society

London 2006

This book is dedicated to the memory of

BRIAN NORTH LEE, FSA
(1936–2007)

Brian North Lee was a prolific author of
books and articles about ex-libris, who
died just as the completed layout was
being sent to the printer. An appreciation
of his life and unrivalled contribution to
the study of bookplates appears in the
March 2007 issue of *Bookplate Journal*

Text © Brian North Lee and
Sir Ilay Campbell of Succoth, Bart.

Published by The Bookplate Society
11 Nella Road, London W6 9PB
2006

450 copies of which 200 are for sale

ISBN 978-0-9555428-0-0

Text and images scanned by
Anthony Pincott and Paul Latcham

Design and page make-up by James Shurmer

Printed by Henry Ling Ltd.,
Dorchester DT1 1HD

The Bookplate Society is an international society
of collectors, bibliophiles, artists and others
dedicated to promoting bookplate use and study.
For details of publications and membership
benefits see page 144 and the Society's website:
www.bookplatesociety.org

Contents

Decretales Epistole Gregorij noni
Pontificis maximi iam recens
plus sexcentis mendis cum
in textu tum in glos-
sis repurga-
te,

B·REMBOLT

Parisijs.

Ex officina Claudij Chevallonij
sub Sole aureo in via ad
diuum Iaco-
bum.

1527. mense Octobri.

s domini Roberti
eid, Abbatis a Kynlos.

Ex libris domini Roberti Reid , Abbatis à Kynlos.

Introduction

It is strange that no-one has until now attempted a chronicling of the history of Scottish ex-libris. Naturally, works on British bookplates have included examples from north of the border, but there is inadequacy in that insofar as a fascinating story was crying out to be told – and it is a tale which deserves a monograph. What it should comprise was the principal question to be faced. The only sensible and helpful answer was ex-libris by Scottish engravers, artists and printers alongside others for Scots produced elsewhere, for all are integral to a balanced survey.

Scotland was slower than England to adopt bookplates as marks of ownership in books. In England there are three recorded examples of the sixteenth century, and probably upwards of 200 in the next; but it was not until the beginning of the eighteenth century that usage took wing – and it did so with surprising alacrity. Favour in earliest times in both countries was for printed book labels, produced at very modest cost and occasionally assuredly as gifts to customers from printers or book-binders. At least 47 English ones can be ascribed to the sixteenth century.

The earliest such labels so far recorded were, however, two Scottish ones, both indicating the ownership of Robert Reid (d. 1558), when Abbot of Kinloss. They were of quite different printing. The single-line one is in a copy of St John Damascene, *Opera*, Basle, 1535, and the other is in a copy of *Decretales Epistole* of Pope Gregory IX, Paris, 1527. Reid became Abbot in 1528, and Bishop of Orkney in 1541, but though he resigned the abbacy to his nephew Walter Reid before 6 April 1553 he apparently still continued to be styled Abbot. In 1538 he had a fire-proof library constructed at Kinloss for a considerable collection of all kinds of literature. In view of his career it seems likely that the two-line label was printed 1528–41 and the other 1535–41 (1).

Printing was, of course, then in its early days, and it was undoubtedly its invention which encouraged the emergence of ex-libris. No two mediaeval manuscripts were precisely similar, but type enabled multiple copies. Some illuminated volumes extended to handsome indication of ownership with arms or dedicatory inscriptions; and hand-painted armorials serving the same purpose occurred in printed books in the early sixteenth century. The painted arms of Cardinal Wolsey (d. 1530) are pasted in a copy of *Tomus Primus Quatuor Conciliorum Generalium*, Paris, 1524, and though there is no proof it was always associated with the book it seems not unlikely (2). There are Scottish examples of the same period. One, dated 1531, declares the ownership of Alexander Mylne, Abbot of Cambuskenneth (3). Another for Bishop William Stewart of Aberdeen is in a book of 1529; and a third, for David Beaton or Bethune (1494–1546) is in a book published in Paris in 1533 (4). Beaton was appointed Archbishop of St Andrews in 1539, and one suspects that the beautifully

(1) *The Bookplate Journal*, Vol. 8, No. 1, March 1990, pp. 44–7.

(2) *British Heraldry*, British Museum Publications, 1978, pp. 72–3; W.J. Hardy, *Book-Plates*, London, 1897, pp. 18, 24 & 26.

(3) *The Bookplate Journal*, New Series. Vol. 3, No. 2, September 2005. Cover, inside cover and pp. 119–23.

(4) Ibid, New Series, Vol. 1, No. 1, March 2003. Cover, inside cover and p. 52.

painted ex-libris was made a little earlier, for it seems to be Paris work and he spent much time there when Bishop of Mirepoix.

We have also to bear in mind that stamps impressed on the boards of books, whether blind or in gold, were at that time and later an option for distinguished people who wished to declare "This book is mine". Most of Reid's books were thus enhanced, but with lettering (5). Beaton's father, James, used an armorial stamp (6). Somewhat later, David Lindsay (*c.*1586–1640), Baron Lindsay of Balcarres, used a couple of book stamps, but so too did others including John Maitland (*c.*1580–1645), who became Earl of Lauderdale (7).

Our concern, though, is marks of ownership actually pasted into books, and so our immediate focus must be on printed labels, of which there were some splendid and intriguing ones as record of early Scottish bibliophiles and other users of them. A number were for individuals, others paid tribute to gifts, and yet more were institutional. Comment on them in that order may be of interest. It is helpful that a goodly number indicate the year of their printing, and most of those are detailed in Lee, *Early Printed Book Labels*, 1976; but in a number of instances printed dates are misleading. A notable example of this is the series of labels for the Chisholms of Stirches in Roxburghshire, which occur dated 1661, 1686, 1705, 1790 and 1808/9. They were almost certainly all printed at the same time as the last of them.

Thomas Nicolson of Aberdeen used three personal labels, one undated and the others 1608 and 1610. The son of James Nicolson, a burgess of Aberdeen, he was an MA, probably of King's College, became an advocate in Edinburgh, was commissary of Aberdeen *c.*1590, made burgess in 1600, and from 1619 was Professor of Civil Law at King's College. He is described in Munro, *Roll of Burgesses*, as of Colbrandspath (Cockburnspath). Edward Raban of Aberdeen (d. 1658) has been said to have printed his labels, and certainly printed others later, but since Raban is only recorded as a printer from 1620 an element of doubt must exist. At that time one cannot believe that labels bearing variant dates were produced for retrospective use. An Englishman, though of German descent, he had an uncle, Peter Raban, who was a clergyman at Melton Mowbray in Leicestershire. After serving in the Dutch wars, Edward worked for a master printer in Leyden and travelled in Germany before settling in Scotland. The first printer in Aberdeen, he became Printer to the Town and University in 1622.

(5) John Duncan & Anthony Ross, *Early Scottish Libraries*, Burne, 1961, pp. 44–7; *Scottish Historical Review*, Vol. 5, pp. 129–31 & Dr. John Stuart, *Records of the Monastery of Kinloss*. preface, p. lv (illustrations).

(6) Cyril Davenport, *English Heraldic Book-Stamps*, London, A. Constable & Co., 1909, p. 61.

(7) Ibid, pp. 269–70 & 277–8. Davenport's *Royal English Bookbindings*, London, Seeley & Co. Ltd., 1896, includes Mary Queen of Scots and James I of England and VI of Scotland.

Another, more ambitiously ornamented label of 1616, also posited as Raban's work, records a gift of "Walterus Balcanquel", i.e. Balcanquhall the elder. Aberdeen and Edinburgh led in label usage, inextensive though it seems to have been for individuals; but Glasgow played its part. A spectacular Aberdeen example is George Anderson's of 1626, which includes the charming phrase "THIS … APPERTAINED UNTO MEE". A space was left for "BIBLE" or "BUIK" to be inserted as appropriate. Anderson was extending to print manuscript wording used earlier to indicate ownership. The earliest seen reads "This Buik pertinis to David Anderson, burges of abd. anno 1573", the second "This buik pertinis to me George Andersone ye Sone to ye David Andersone". "Appertaineth to" also occurs in the manuscript inscription on the Gilbert Hervie Bible at Aberdeen, illustration of which follows, and it also contains a Raban label dated 1631.

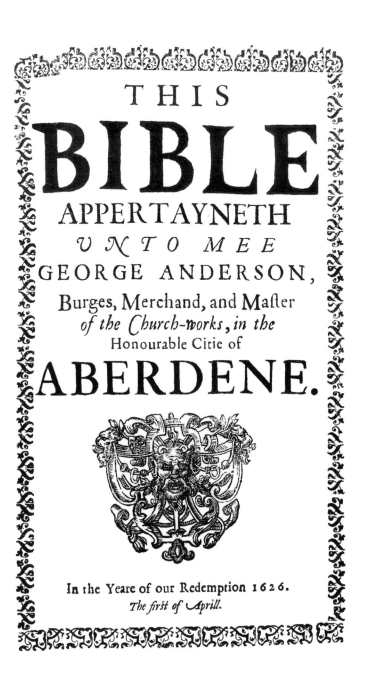

There is, amongst others, an undated printed label (Viner Collection) which reads 'This Book appertaineth unto the calling of the Wrights of Glasgow". They formed one of the fourteen incorporations of the Trades of Glasgow and were originally united with the Masons and Coopers. It seems unlikely that they had a library and the label was probably used for their minute books.

A label in a book in the Town House, Dunbar reads "M. William Arthure aucht this book", and one assumes that "aucht" indicates "owneth". It is in a *Hebrew Bible*, Hamburg, 1587. William Arthur, MA (d. 1654 aged about 82) was admitted to the charge of Corstorphine 8 June 1599, but in the same year a complaint was made that he was "overleirnit a man for thame". He nevertheless continued with a lively career (see *Fasti Ecclesiae Scoticanae*, 1915, Vol. 1, pp. 6, 95 & 100). Other interesting early Scottish users of labels included the laird and poet William Drummond of Hawthornden, whose label reads "GVILIELMVS DRVMMONDVS ab Hawthornden", but there is not space to expand on it here.

A later printed label of 1768, illustration of which follows, also belonged to a Cockburnspath resident, Robert Nisbet, and it is an unusually large one for its date. Though the inscription signifies that it was for his Bible he may have had the Old and New Testaments separately bound, for it occurs in black and in red. It was customary, but more especially in England, for visitors to printing shops to be offered a keepsake. Some such ended up as book labels, for they really had no other practical use, and more precisely designated ones were probably an alternative. Their full story will remain elusive, however, for in the process of rebinding books over subsequent centuries ex-libris on old boards were often discarded.

Turning now to gifts to institutions, there was a most intriguing variant to a book label *per se*: the "catalogus librorum". This not only marked gifts but detailed the books it included. There is one of 1617 recording the donation of 26 volumes from William Rig of Mortoun to Edinburgh University. Other instances are John Craw, a merchant burgess of Edinburgh, who gave 34 volumes in 1637, Henry Wardlaw who gave 48 in 1638, and Robert Johnston who bequeathed 172 in 1640. The Nairn bequest of 1678 was more ambitious, and was published as a book prefaced by a life of its donor. The earliest example, though, was English not Scottish, and records a gift by William Wickham, Bishop of Lincoln, to King's College, Cambridge. James Raith, of Edmonstone House. Dalkeith, gave books to Edinburgh in 1625, marked by an ambitious label, but though similar generosities were occasionally similarly commemorated, it seems that the Scottish universities early on never developed the tradition which had been familiar at Oxford and Cambridge from the late sixteenth century.

Scottish armorial bookplates emerged in the seventeenth century, and though they were disparate in composition the term Early Armorial is generally apt. Some examples of the period were probably engravings made for another purpose, which may or may not have served in books, and the nation's waste not want not sense of carefulness may have been a factor. It is certainly true to say that elegance of engraving was not always a priority, the artificer's zeal being more marked than sweetness of line. Naturally, as elsewhere in Britain then and since, a great many bookplates were unsigned by their engravers, and the earliest it is possible to name are those who contributed to Alexander Nisbet's *Heraldic Plates* (8). They included Archibald Burden, son of James Burden and his wife Margaret Drummond, said to have been daughter of James, Earl of Perth – but she may have been

(8) See Andrew Ross & Francis J. Grant, *Alexander Nisbet's Heraldic Plates*, Edinburgh, George Waterston & Sons, 1892.

Mr John Birnie of Broomhill

illegitimate, for her name does not appear in printed genealogies of the family. Of the Burdens of Feddal, he was described in the Nisbet book, above, as "Goldsmith and Engraver in Edinburgh" but was probably more precisely a goldsmith's engraver, and he worked with variable success. What is clear – and the George Craufurd plate shows it – is that he was conversant with the heraldic style then prevalent in England. Robert Mylne, C. Norton and Robert Wood were contemporaries similarly engaged, and a print of the last's armorial for John Birnie in the Hall Crouch Collection at the Society of Antiquaries instances how, if required, a large print was trimmed to be accommodated in a book. Handsomeness was diminished, and the engraver's signature, "Rt. Wood Sculpst", lost, excepting its end at lower left. Wood was an engraver in Edinburgh 1710–51. The Riddell of Kinglass plate is a Scottish example of a misleading ex-libris date – in this case 1639 – for it was certainly eighteenth century, as the notes which follow indicate.

Scotland was a very poor country in the sixteenth and seventeenth centuries, a situation which didn't encourage or assist the building up of personal libraries. Despite James VI's accession, the kingdoms continued to operate separately; Scottish traders suffered from the forceful methods of English competition, encouraged or engineered by the Government; and matters came to a head with the "Darian Adventure"; and the financial disaster for many Scotsmen eventually won the support of influential Scottish noblemen for Union of the Parliaments.

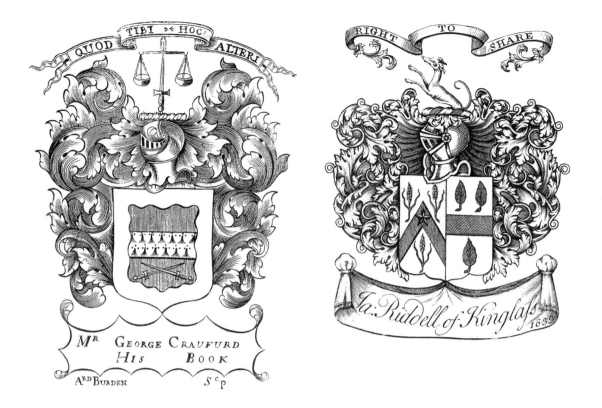

Though Scotland lacked a William Jackson, he played some part in its bookplate history. A London engraver working near the Inns of Court, he popularised usage in the years around 1700 by actively seeking clients. Selecting principally landed people and the nobility, he seems to have proffered prints of their arms in hope of their acceptance for use in books – and his geographical range included Scotland. His workshop produced in excess of 635 ex-libris, and nothing more encourages would-be commissioners than seeing attractive artefacts which others possess.

Had there been a law that bookplates be signed, and ideally dated, by their creators we should have been much the wiser, but the vast majority were unsigned. In some cases we can attribute authorship on stylistic grounds. Elsewhere it can be a fallible pursuit. Everywhere in the British Isles such works were almost entirely the work of trade engravers until the latter part of the nineteenth century. In England the lump was leavened by the participation of William Faithorne the elder, William Hogarth, Francesco Bartolozzi and similar luminaries. That never appertained in Scotland, so there are few early ex-libris which are notably remarkable works of art. The greatest output was understandably from Edinburgh, but Aberdeen, Stirling, Glasgow, Leith and other sizeable centres of population played their part in the history of the trade. In addition to Burden, Mylne, Norton and Wood, Thomas Calder was working 1710–20, probably in Edinburgh. Thomas Forbes of Aberdeen signed a couple of bookplates a decade later, Andrew Johnston, probably of Edinburgh, was bookplate making 1720–40, and George Main of Edinburgh (he and Forbes are not illustrated here) signed half a dozen ex-libris 1700–40. The period witnessed the vogue for Early Armorial and then Jacobean compositions. Our ex-libris stylistic terminologies were devised by the Hon. Leicester Warren (9), and though they

(9) The Hon. J. Leicester Warren, *A Guide to the Study of Book-plates*, London, John Pearson, 1880; second edition (as Lord de Tabley, but published posthumously), Manchester, Sherratt & Hughes, 1900.

The Right Honble John, Lord
Colvill of Culross.

were less than ideal, indeed rather misleading, they have persisted and will no doubt continue to do so.

The most usual characteristics of Early Armorials were a squarish shield, with helm, crest and rich mantling. The Birnie and Craufurd armorials illustrate the point, though it should be added that the mantling of the former is a delightful *tour de force*. One could wish for similar ability in respect of the lettering, which is lamentable. The same criticism applies, incidentally, to the Earl of Wigton and Erskine of Dun armorials which follow, and others.

At this point it may be useful to make one or two observations about arms and their accompaniments. In England, sons are indicated by a mark of cadency – label, crescent, mullet, martlet, etc., on the upper part of the arms. In Scotland, bordures with different tinctures, partitions or sub-charges take their place. Mottoes, often on a ribbon, can in England be changed at will (and frequently are), but in Scotland they are technically subject to armorial control, not always observed. They are specified on patents and must be re-matriculated with arms. Supporters, aside the arms, or sometimes behind them, go back in armorial usage to the fifteenth century at least, and some of the Scottish ones featured amongst the illustrations here are fascinating. Since the matter is complicated, let us focus here just on Scotland, where they are granted on the authority of Lord Lyon to peers, baronets, knights grand cross of the orders of chivalry, chiefs of clans, certain knights and the heirs of minor barons who sat in Parliament prior to 1587 as of right. The heir apparent can use his father's supporters. A royal warrant can enable supporters to someone not normally entitled to them, and certain families may claim an ancient right to use supporters (10). From the point of view of symmetry it can be more pleasing if they are a pair of similarly-sized creatures, but exceptions can be beguiling and fun. A particularly curious instance is the rhinoceros supporter on Lord Colvill of Culross's plate. His fellow supporter is a Hercules – not to be confused with the wild men who so often feature elsewhere on Scottish armorials, displaying machismo albeit sometimes rather quaintly. The rhino seems to be wearing breeks and doublet.

(10) See Stephen Friar, *A New Dictionary of Heraldry*, A & C Black, London, 1987, pp. 330–33.

The Jacobean style was so named because of its ornament's similarity to ecclesiastical woodwork, mouldings, map cartouches and suchlike of the late seventeenth century. It flourished in England and Scotland for over 40 years from *c.*1700, but the character it took often differed significantly. Yet there were always exceptions, not least north of the border. In England the cartouche tended to predominate, and very beautiful some were, with charming scroll work, etc. Scots tended to prefer to retain the helm, with light rather horizontal mantling aside it. Fish-scale or lattice backgrounds were familiar, as were brackets as alternative or adjunct to a cartouche. Script rather than upright lettering was also popular. Scottish Jacobeans like the John Finlaysone and George Wishart plates had pleasing elegance. Others, including the Dalrymple, display ambition more coarsely. The last is also a nice instance of the point made above about the compatability of supporters, for either the lion is miniscule or the falcon disguised as a parrot would put a roc to shame.

Oval Jacobeans also had some favour, and amongst several which follow a particularly quaint and unusual example belonged to Charles Maitland, 6th Earl of Lauderdale. Had it not been precisely dated 1716 one would suppose it to have been earlier; but its especial interest is that it was cut on wood or soft metal. Though poorly inked and printed, it deserves inclusion both on that account and because many Scottish ex-libris less than strictly conformed to fashion, and are the more interesting for it. Cuts on wood or metal were a minority option for bookplate making throughout Britain, and there are fewer Scottish than English examples; but amongst instances noted are a spade shield armorial with supporters for Lockhart of Cleghorn, an anonymous Wedderburn plate with similar components, and an Early Armorial for Wilson of Finzeauch (F.32052) which appears to be older than it is because of its crude cutting. The last of them, incidentally, evidences a difficulty for the bookplate scholar in respect of the rendering of place names in inscriptions. You will not find Finzeauch in contemporary gazetteers, but it corresponds to Finshaugh in Monymusk, Aberdeenshire, a village about 20 miles north-west of Aberdeen. Such puzzles are not infrequently encountered, and can add a little piquancy to the patient sleuthing which forms part of serious ex-libris research.

The essence of the so-called Chippendale, or rococo, bookplate is lack of symmetry, and a lightness of composition which seems to discard the laws of gravity. Perhaps its freedom and gay exuberance was not exactly to Scottish taste but, whether or no, its interpretation and personality north of the border was distinctly individual. This style emerged towards the end of the 1730s, was in full spate in England by 1755, and thereafter in the same became ever more wanton and excrescence-orientated. Perhaps it was because so many Scots were sons of the kirk that their bookplate engravers literally cut it down to size in physical and ornamental terms. It is pleasing to add, though, that what resulted could and sometimes did evince great charm. What was so impressive, and ground-breaking, was that the strength of line and boldness of earlier styles was replaced by a delicacy of cutting on occasion pronouncedly finicky. In some examples profuse leafiness held sway; elsewhere there could be vibrant busyness. One excludes the Thomas Carnegy of Craigo plate which follows (and others which don't), for that was certainly engraved in England, and is of a familiar stock pattern. The John Callander is, by contrast, characterfully Scottish, and almost certainly the work of Richard Cooper, who is also represented later on. It is worth adding that whilst some Scots have over the centuries turned to English bookplate makers, sometimes because of travels or residence in the south, Scottish engravers were not infrequently called upon by clients south of the border during the Chippendale period and later.

John Finlaysone

Mʳ George Wiſhart Miniſter of the Trone Church of Edinburgh.

Sir Henᵧ Dalrymple of Northberwick Baronet Lord preſident of the Seſsion

John Callander of Craigforth Advocate

DO OR DIE

Archibald Douglas

George Goldie
Edin.

Nº

John Edmiston
GLASGOW

AVISE LA FINE

Robert Kennedy Esq.
of Auchtyfardel

Though there were exceptions, such as the 1768 Nisbet printed label already cited, Scots who sought labels in that period mostly plumped for engraved ones, and they are markedly numerous. It is not difficult to explain. Scottish pictorials rarely occurred until much later, and for non-armigerous people who were proud of their books, and probably of their trades and careers, book labels were the only option. Maybe the impossibility of attribution to owner in most cases has led to their neglect by collectors, but many are very endearing and in view of their usage they are more than a mere footnote to bookplate history. Ex-libris aficionados tend to belong to one of two camps: those for whom armory and the lineage of families is the draw, and others whose fascination is the graphic tale personal marks of ownership afford and inform. They deserve to co-exist side by side, being complementary.

As fashions change, as is inevitable periodically, one observes that the successor joyfully portrays reaction to what went before. So it was when Chippendale compositions had had their day – and quite a long one it had been. Arms in spade-shaped shields became popular from c.1775, and remained so for the next quarter of a century. Curiously, their story was the reverse of that of rococo designs. As already indicated, the latter developed, except in chaste Scotland, with increasing elaboration. Spade shield plates were initially adorned with wreaths, festoons or both, but some years later, rather mystifyingly, the ornament was pared back. Indeed, some coppers were reworked, which seems a retrograde step for a style which began its career so beautifully and elegantly. Some Scottish examples testify to it, but we must bear in mind that throughout Britain the commissioning of ex-libris was experiencing a temporary lull. One reason for it may well have been that plenty of daddy's plates were still in the drawer and could be turned to use, altered or unchanged. Change could be effected by cutting off inscriptions at the base of armorials, paternal arms remaining the same. Manuscript amendments also saved a few pennies, and one wishes there were more of them, for the best can be very informative.

The Trustees of the National Library of Scotland

One of the most interesting aspects of Scottish spade shields is that they had drawn so close in character to English ones that apart from the name, and sometimes the character of the cutting, only the names and inscriptions are sure evidence of to where they appertained. The Sir Henry Hay Makdougall, and others which follow, display something of the range of the style's diversity and make one wish that its popularity had continued longer.

From the years of rococo popularity, if we study signed ex-libris for evidence of sizeable individual or workshop production, certain engravers stand out for comment. The Hector Gavins, father and son, of Edinburgh, were prolific 1760–1830, James and Robert Kirkwood, father and son, were active in Edinburgh in the first decades of the nineteenth century, and so were Daniel and William Home Lizars of the same 1800–52. They likewise were father and son, and in that indicate flourishing businesses as well as the draw of the "family firm". Also in Edinburgh, Charles Thomson was active 1800–30, and Joseph Swan was a counterpart in Glasgow 1820–40. When in 1823 the great wood engraver Thomas Bewick visited Edinburgh for the second time, he recorded that he paid his "respects to the son and successor of my kind friend of former years, the late Mr. Hector Gavin, and the same to the sons and successors of the late Mr. D. Lizars. All these, in my estimation, were doing credit to their instruction as engravers" (11). That was no small praise from such a giant. It indicates, of course, that William Home Lizars had a brother or brothers in the family business, but more importantly implies that engravers met socially and no doubt also "talked shop". We tend, evidence being scant, to see them as separate cohabitants of a place, but there must everywhere have been significant interaction, not least in regard to apprentices and their subsequent careers.

Throughout much of the nineteenth century the so-called die-sinker armorials predominated. One could obtain them almost anywhere of town size, they tended to be well-cut armorials, often engraved on steel, and they became ubiquitous. It seems that if you were a "gentleman" you required a library and thus an ex-libris. Nor was entitlement to arms a deterrent, for those of people of the same surname were often adopted. The Lyon Court would have been inundated with work in bringing such people to heel. A consequent snag for collectors can thus be impossibility of attribution; but few have cherished die-sinkers, their weakness being lack of artistic inspiration and flair. Amongst pleasant exceptions is the Pringle of Clifton armorial by the Lizars. It followed, as night does day, that reiterated compositions became an easy option for engravers. J & J. Johnstone of Edinburgh produced numerous ex-libris, and you will see that the James Boyd crest plate's ornament at base echoes that of the Pringle. It was, moreover, one of a small Johnstone group which differ scarcely at all. The same was true of the composition by Scott and Ferguson for Dr. Paterson. Stock patterns have a history going back to the early eighteenth century, but something of their appeal diminished when engraved on steel on the treadmill of nineteenth century commercial go-getting. Yet it would be unfair to blame the engravers since it is ultimately the client who decides whether or not to have a plate unique to him or herself.

Scottish bibliophiles very rarely chose pictorial ex-libris until the latter part of the nineteenth century. Several notable exceptions are shown here, and the first for comment is the quaint design featuring a portrait of Boerhaave, engraved by Patrick Begbie, and one of three distinctly idiosyn-cratic ex-libris (the others follow) used by Dr John Boswell, who studied medicine under Boerhaave

(11) Quoted in George Herbert Bushnell, *Scottish Engravers*. OUP, 1949, p. 19, but see Bewick's *Memoir*, any edition, for an account of his Scottish trips.

Sᵣ Henry Hay Makdougall
Barᵗ of Makerstoun

CONFIDO.

James Boyd. LL.D.

Dᵣ Paterson,
32, Charlotte Street, LEITH.

at Leyden. Another is Andrew Lumisden's very individual plate by his brother-in-law Sir Robert Strange, who was knighted by George III in 1787.

From about 1860 in Britain there was considerable advance in the incidence of pictorials, and book illustrators were amongst those who wrought the change, even though many of them limited their endeavours to plates of people close to them. In that context, William Bell Scott was a Scotsman of marked interest to us. He was the seventh son of the engraver Robert Scott of Edinburgh, who incidentally made a pictorial-armorial plate for the Cupar Library in Fife. It is arguable that William was amongst the earliest collectors of ex-libris north of the border. Though de Tabley made no acknowledgement to him in his *Guide* – the pioneer work on British bookplates – the anonymous *In Memoriam* of him states that "under the influence of Mr William Bell Scott (he) began to collect bookplates". Scott was therefore clearly an inspirer. We know little of the character of his holdings, but in a letter of 14 March 1890 to James Roberts Brown, a founder member and officer of the Ex Libris Society, he wrote: "I once had a large collection. Of late I kept those only used by celebrated men, as you wd see in the small portfolio at my sale the other day". In addition , William Bell Scott made ex-libris for ten people, mostly or perhaps all friends, and they are charming works, not least because they are so evocative of their period (12).

Bookplate collecting quietly gained momentum for years before the Ex Libris Society was founded in 1891, and artificers of other than die-sinkers were multiplying. Indeed, so much was happening that summarising its strands is impossible here. At its heart, though, lay a genuine desire for a renaissance of bookplate art and design. Charles William Sherborn and George W. Eve developed that professionally in England with their engraved or etched armorials. Everywhere in Britain there was a burgeoning of amateur designers, not a few of whom were notably inadequate. One can have too much of homely portrayals, pseudo-mediaevalism or twee excursions into what the Victorians discerned as wit. Scotland wasn't very different from elsewhere in that transitional period, but in retrospect three developments can be described as important. Herald painters and their collaborators at the Lyon Court, to which we shall turn shortly, were bringing heraldic compositions back into their own; indigenous artists had started to display sheer excellence; and Edinburgh was to witness an extension of bookplate literature.

The artists in question included the Glasgow "boys and girls", whose works are now so highly esteemed. Charles Rennie Mackintosh has achieved cult status, and one wishes ex-libris design had been amongst his preoccupations. It was for Jessie M. King, and a drawing by her for a bookplate sold for £2,250 some years ago. Annie French was also of the group, and very fine her work is too. Since most of their ex-libris were made for friends it is unlikely that they were generally seen as innovators for some time, but their very involvement is indicative of reappraisal of the potential of the art. Then there was the bookplate making of Sir David Young Cameron and his sister Katharine, Mrs Kay, who were both etchers. He probably created more marks of book ownership than any other topographical etcher during his time and since. There was also his close friend Joseph W. Simpson, who though born in Carlisle studied art in Edinburgh and later worked for publishers there.

The publisher of especial relevance to us was Otto Schulze. His books were limited editions, are hard to come by now, and are rarely found on exlibrists' shelves – partly because of their cost but also

(12) *The Bookplate Journal*, Vol. 4, No. 1, March 1986, pp. 3–19: "William Bell Scott's place in bookplate history".

HAROLD·NELSON HIS·BOOK·OF·BOOKPLATES·CONSISTING OF 24·ORIGINAL·DESIGNS

PVBLISHED·1904·BY
OTTO·SCHVLZE&COMPANY
20·SOVTH·FREDERICK·
STREET·&·EDINBVRGH·

since they lack the documentation which would be a *sine qua non* nowadays. Schulze published *David Beckett: his book of bookplates*, 1906, *Charles E. Dawson: his book of bookplates*, 1907, *James Guthrie: his book of bookplates*, 1907, *Harold Nelson: his book of bookplates*, 1904 (the title-page of which is shown here), *Reproductions of twenty-five (Nelson) designs for bookplates*, 1910, *J. W. Simpson: his book of bookplates*, n.d, and *The Book-lovers Magazine*, 1900–09. Schulze's venture was markedly ambitious, and unparalleled during its time in featuring individual contemporary artists; for it wasn't until a decade later that James Guthrie – the son, incidentally, of a Glasgow metal merchant – embarked on bookplate texts in England somewhat after the same mould. Such bold enterprises were part of the reaction against overdue concentration on the historical side of the subject which the Ex Libris Society favoured and which Gleeson White remonstrated against in his "*Modern book-plates and their designers*", the Studio special winter number 1898–9. Otto Schulze's life seems elusive, but there was a strong German protestant presence in Edinburgh from *c.*1870 and it was still in evidence during the years he was working.

Schulze was more interested in the artists he featured than where they lived, and it is clear that national borders impinged little on ex-libris commissioning in the early decades of the twentieth century. Scots gravitated to England, or occasionally to America, France or elsewhere for artificers who could provide what they required. From 1900 the finest Scottish practitioners available for commissions tended to be armorial designers. The best of them did work for or were herald painters at the Court of Lord Lyon in Edinburgh – and the qualification calls for definition. Lyon Court has at any one time only one designated "herald painter" but understandably employs artists more widely. Since 1898 they have been: Graham Johnston until 1927, Alfred George Law Samson until 1943, Herbert Lewis Gordon until 1947, Nora Mary Gordon until 1959, Katherine Chart until 1967, Mary Jane Gordon (later Murray) until 1974, and Jennifer Mitchell (later Phillips) since then. Beryl Tittensor and Patricia Bertram have also lent their talents to Lyon Office work and designing bookplates. The finest early ones were Johnston and Law Samson, and collectors have tended to prefer the former, for his output was much more considerable. No-one has yet produced a complete checklist of his plates, but they were certainly in excess of 160. He could on occasion be a plagiarist, but that palls into insignificance in view of his quality. The Macbeth plate is one of his finest. He has also inspired armorial designs ever since, and that could be seen as a criticism, but not of him. There has been in Britain a tendency for heraldic depictions to become increasingly sparing in respect of mantling and ornament, but whilst the only essential is correct armory many people naturally desire compositions including a measure of heraldic bravura and appropriate decoration. Even traditional symbols such as thistles, roses or maple leaves can say their bit, but so too can other motifs if not too crowded. It seems sad that some of today's artists have to turn back upwards of a century for models, there having been a paucity of innovation since. In Johnston's case there is a degree of irony in his later acclaim, for it is clear that when working he felt undervalued. He advertised diligently, both directly and by sending so much work for inclusion in the *Ex-Libris Journal* post-1900 that Johnston creations tend to dominate; and he despised the heraldry of many of the engravers used by J & E. Bumpus, even going so far as to write to the King in hopes of commissioning. He nevertheless dominates in that golden age of Scottish armory, and other countrymen not yet mentioned who were major figures during it include Archibald S. Leslie and John R. Sutherland.

Some Scottish ex-libris of the period were drawings reproduced by line-block; others were achieved by photolithography or comparable techniques; others were etched or engraved but, in line

EX—LIBRIS ★
WILLIAM·GILCHRIST
·MACBETH·

Ex Libris

GIARDINO DEI BOBOLI

AGNES DUNLOP

KATHLEEN FINLAY

HORSMAN

with custom then, some artificers remained anonymous. They were, anyhow, mostly facsimile interpreters. Several Scottish engravers of previous times made their mark far from home. Two American instances call for mention. Samuel Allardyce, or Allerdice (b. *c.*1760), was apprenticed to Robert Scott (see p. 20), but moved to Philadelphia, where he became die-sinker to the USA Mint. He engraved a label for the Library Company of Baltimore. Alexander Anderson (1775–1870) was born in New York of Scottish parents, and became the first American wood engraver, called the American Bewick. Four ex-libris by him are on wood, and three on copper; he could be very fine; and impressively he was engraving illustrations for Barbour's *Historical Collections of New Jersey* aged 93. Francis Legat (1755–1809) was born in Scotland, became a pupil of Andrew Bell of Edinburgh, but he went to London in 1780 and made his career there working for Boydell and other publishers. His acclaimed ex-libris are the two states of the Anna Damer plate, designed by Agnes Berry. Had we but world enough and time – and space – more engravers than feature could have been included, but a sizeable number of those who stayed to make their careers in Scotland limited themselves to one or two signed bookplates.

To a very significant extent ex-libris history has been preserved by collectors, and the greatest one relevant here was Dr. John Henderson Smith, who bequeathed his remarkable assemblage to the National Library of Scotland in 1952. He lived at Harpenden in Hertfordshire, belonged to the Ex Libris Society, and was secretary of the Bookplate Exchange Club 1901–48. It was the secretary's privilege to have first choice of the plates sent for exchange, and Henderson Smith took full advantage of it, especially in respect of early Scottish examples. The years and long period of his activity were instrumental to his success, for so many old rarities which were available then are scarcely encountered now. The Rev. Dr. John Lamb, of New College Mound, Edinburgh, was also a member of the Club 1950–67. Both of the above concentrated on armorial plates, as mostly have the significant but not numerous collectors since. An exception was the delightful Elizabeth Kyle (Agnes Dunlop), of Ayr, the novelist, newspaper correspondent, and recorder of the character of her times. Her enthusiasm was for artistry rather than armory, and her bookplate was engraved on wood by William MacLaren, who had been a pupil of Joan Hassall whilst she was teaching in Edinburgh during the Second World War. During that period Joan engraved a bookplate for Kathleen Finlay Horsman in the same medium which was an absolute delight but proved impossible for adequate commercial production. It was a four-colour block, and printers simply couldn't get the colour balance right – so it ended up for use printed in black alone.

Examples of other ex-libris made in Scotland during the last century follow. It was a period which saw great variety artistically, but, excepting strictly heraldic designs at their best, the overall picture has some curate's egg characteristics. If we study the output of major English figures in that *oeuvre* we find that the creations of some of them run into hundreds, but Scotland lacked counterparts to such as J. A. C. Harrison, Robert Osmond, George Friend, Reynolds Stone, Leo Wyatt and Simon Brett. Almost all of them have had clients north of the border – for one turns elsewhere if there is no-one nearer home to supply demand. We may hope that the situation soon changes, for graphic artists are numerous and highly skilled throughout the length of the land. As we have tried to illustrate here, the history of ex-libris art in Scotland was for so long a vigorous and impressive business. It deserves handsome extension, and hopefully soon.

Acknowledgements

We owe thanks to a number of people for assistance and information during research for this book: Iain Bain, William Bell, Charles John Burnett, Ross Herald, David Burnett, Gemma Corby of the University of Aberdeen historical collections, special libraries and archives, Clare and the late Niall Devitt, Peter de Vere Beauclerk-Dewar, Mrs M. E. Frost, Dr Stanley Hanuman, Mrs R. M. Hart, archivist at St Andrews University, Paul Latcham, John Malden, Bridget McConnell of Glasgow City Council, Ian Marshall, President of the Glasgow Archaeological Society, Angela Lemaire, Christopher Morgan, librarian of the Faculty of Actuaries, Edinburgh, Peter Drummond-Murray of Mastrick, Slains Pursuivant, Anthony Pincott, Mrs Carol Primrose, Mrs Elizabeth Roads, Carrick Pursuivant and Lyon Clerk, Richard Shirley Smith, Mrs Amoret Tanner, Christopher Thompson, Ian Wallace, James Wilson, and Jeremy and Gill Wilyman. Gratitude is also due to The Town House, Aberdeen and the City Engineer's Department for a photograph of the Gilbert Hervie Bible inscription. It must, however, be understood that any errors in this book are entirely the responsibility of its authors.

Picture Credits

The majority of illustrations for this book were scanned from original ex-libris in the authors' collections. Recourse to the Ex Libris Journal was necessary in the case of the Ildephonsus Kennedy ex-libris, and two images had to be reproduced from photocopies. Acknowledgements and grateful thanks for assistance with the provision of scans or loan of ex-libris are owed to the following: Bodleian Library, Oxford (John Johnson Collection); British Museum Department of Prints and Drawings (Franks and Viner Collections); The Fitzwilliam Museum, Cambridge; Liverpool Central Library; The National Library of Scotland (Henderson Smith Collection); Anthony Pincott; The Estate of John Simpson; Society of Antiquaries of London (Hall Crouch Collection); James L. Wilson; and Jem Wilyman.

Notes on the cover illustrations and bookplates which precede the catalogue

FRASER OF LEDECLUNE
(Front cover illustration and p. 33)

Quarterly armorial, etc. Sgd: L, for John Leighton, it was process reproduced and occurs on buff, orange, blue and crimson paper, and printed on white paper in black, red and pale brown (F.11250–54 are amongst them). See pp. 117–118 for another bookplate used by the same owner, and for biographical details. John Leighton (1822–1912), who called himself "Luke Limner", was an artist, illustrator, book decorator and from at least 1849 a designer of ex-libris. He became a vice-president of the Ex Libris Society. See *Bookplate Collecting in Britain*, 1991, pp. 4–5.

Sr James Primerose of Carington Baronet
(Frontispiece)

Large single coat Early Armorial. Sgd: Rot. Wood sculp. F.24174. Alexander Nisbet, the heraldic writer, published the first volume of his *System of Heraldry* in 1722 (see *British Bookplates*, 1979, p. 48). The coppers went to the people to whom they appertained, and several of them were used by their owners as bookplates despite their large size. A print of this plate, together with Sir James's signature, belonged to John Orr, and G. H. Viner had another in a copy of *The Acts & Orders of the Meeting of the Estates of the Kingdom of Scotland, etc.*, 1690, pasted on the verso of the title-page. Sir James Primerose of Carrington (d. 1706), second son of Sir William Primerose, was MP for Edinburghshire in 1702. This armorial must predate his creation as Viscount Primerose on 30 November 1703. He married Lady Eleanor Campbell, youngest daughter of James, 2nd Earl of Loudoun. She married later John Dalrymple, 2nd Earl of Stair, and died in 1759. In view of the above, readers will realise that Sir James could not have possessed the copper, being long dead when the book came out. It seems reasonable to suppose that he was sent prints as baronet and put several of them in his books. Robert Wood (fl. 1700–22) was an engraver in Edinburgh, and his best-known print was of Sir George Mackenzie. Other bookplates by him were for George Balderston, John Birnie (see below), and

Plenderleith of BIyth. Wood subscribed to Nisbet's *Essay on … Armories*, 1718 as well as engraving plates used in the 1722 volume.

Ex Libris Frederick Fothringham Macdonald of Lochlands *(Title-page illustration)*

Single coat armorial. Sgd: GJ 1905, and thus the work of Graham Johnston. Collotype. Frederick Fothringham Macdonald (b. 1848), of Lochlands, Angus and Cliff House, Arbroath, was the son of John Macdonald and Anne his wife, daughter of William Kid. Arms matriculated 1905. His elder brother, William Kid Macdonald, recorded his arms at Lyon Office in 1894. Graham Johnston (1869–1927), the son of James M. Johnston, an Edinburgh printer, studied graphic design in London and then joined Scott and Ferguson, engravers in Edinburgh. On the advice of Balfour Paul, who became Lord Lyon in 1890, he became a pupil of John Forbes Nixon, and he was then herald painter at the Lyon Court 1898–1927. His uncle, John Lawson Johnston (1839–1900), who recorded arms at Lyon Office in 1897, was the inventor of Bovril.

Ex libris domini Roberti Reid, Abbatis a Kynlos *(p. 6)*

These one-line and two-line labels are discussed on p. 7. See also *The Bookplate Journal*, March 1990, pp. 44–7.

Mr. THOMAS NICOLSON. COM. 1610. ABD. *(p. 8)*

It seems to have been Nicolson's preference to paste his labels at the bottom of title-pages, and that no doubt accounts for the trimming of their handsome borders when it proved necessary. See *Early Printed Book Labels*, 1976, pp. 18–19 & 21–22.

THIS BIBLE APPERTAINETH UNTO MEE GEORGE ANDERSON, etc. *(p. 9)*

This occurs in a copy of *The Bible in English*, 1550, printed by Whitchurch, now in the library at Harvard University. See *Early Printed Book Labels*, 1976, pp. 33–4. George Anderson (or Andersone) was the elder son of William Andersone. He was admitted burgess of Aberdeen on 6 January 1616. In 1628 he was charged with others before the Privy Council with having written and uttered certain pasquils, including one against the Provost of Aberdeen. On subsequently denying the charge on oath he was assoilzied. Anderson died after 27 June 1638. His wife, Jean, who had earlier been the wife of Robert Mar, burgess of Aberdeen, was the daughter of Alexander Chalmers of Cults, who was sometime Provost.

Mr John Birnie of Broomhill *(p. 11)*

Large single coat armorial by Robert Wood (for comment on whom see Primrose, above), cut down to fit into a book too narrow to accommodate it. Hall Crouch Collection. John Birnie (b. 1674) was the son of John Birnie, who was born at Houston in 1643. He was born at Caerlaverock, and was served heir to his father 15 July 1727. In 1702 he married Elizabeth, the daughter of Alexander Frogg, merchant in Edinburgh, but she died in 1716 aged 39, having borne him a number of children.

MR GEORGE CRAUFURD HIS BOOK *(p. 12)*

Early single coat armorial, interesting in that its wording suggests its owner favoured the wording of printed labels. Sgd: ARD BURDEN SCUP. F.7260. George Craufurd, or Crawford (b. 1684) was the second son of Thomas Craufurd, 1st of Cartsburn (b. 1631), who matriculated these arms at Lyon Office 1672–7 He became a genealogist and historian, was author of *Scottish Peerage* and *The Shire of Renfrew*, and died 1748. Archibald Burden (see p. 10) engraved a number of bookplates in addition to this one. Sir Robert Blackwood of Pittrevie Lo(r)d Provost of Edinburgh, the Erskine of Dun and Birnie of Broomhill plates, which follow. Fincham's list of his works needs the following additions: Buchanan of that Ilk, Mr. Hew Craufurd Writer to the Signet (F.7261), an anonymous mantle plate for the Duke of Hamilton, Maule of Kellie, and The Viscount of Garnock. That Franks possessed only one of them indicates their rarity. On stylistic grounds one can also add that the unsigned armorial in the same style for Martin Eccles Doctor of Medicine Edinr. (F.9517) was also almost certainly of his making.

Jas Riddell of Kinglass 1639 *(p. 12)*

Jacobean impaled coat armorial. NIF. This is arguably the most difficult Scottish bookplate to document, for its character and the unequivocal date leave so many questions unanswered. Whilst on stylistic grounds it couldn't be seventeenth century, the impalement is the problem, for it is Foulis. James Riddell of Kinglass (d. 1674) married Elizabeth, daughter of George Foulis of Ravelston, Esq., Master of the King's Mint (Burke gives James as her father's name). There is an article by R. Garraway Rice on this bookplate in the *Ex-Libris Journal*, Vol. 1, 1891, pp. 77–8, in which he concluded after discussion that it was not engraved later than 1674. One simply cannot believe it. Admittedly, Riddell married in 1639, and commemoration of that may have occasioned the year cited in the inscription. Perhaps a descendant had the plate engraved to mark books in the library which had once been his. Collectors in the classic period seemed clear about the plate's comparative unimportance. In the Julian Marshall auction of 1906 a print of the large Aikman of Cairnie comprised a single lot and raised £3.3.0d. The Riddell, by contrast, though it had eluded Franks was simply one of a lot (784) of 33 plates which sold for only £2.2.0d. It was clearly recognised for what it was, and wasn't.

The Rt. Honble. the Lord Colvill of Culross *(p. 13)*

Quarterly coat Jacobean armorial with supporters. F.6562. John, 6th Lord Colville of Culross (1689–1741) was an ensign in the army in the Cameronian Regiment, and was at the battle of Malplaquet and the siege of Mons. He fought for the Government during the 1715 Jacobite rising, and in 1722 was served heir to 2nd Lord Colville, but it was a year later that the Committee of Privileges found him entitled to the dignity of Lord Colville of Culross. He then served in Gibraltar and was Lieutenant-Colonel commanding a batallion in America, and was present at the siege of Carthagena. In 1716 he married Elizabeth Johnston, who survived him. Colville was the eldest son of Alexander, of Kincardine (1666–1717), *de jure* 5th Lord, who never claimed or assumed the title.

John Finlaysone *(p. 15)*

Quarterly coat Jacobean armorial. F.10532. The arms are Finlaysone quartering Borthwick, with a crescent for difference. They are not recorded at Lyon Office but are in *Burke's General Armory*.

Mr. George Wishart Minister of the Trone Church of Edinburgh *(p. 15)*

Single coat Jacobean armorial. F.32286. The original copper for this bookplate is in the collection of Iain Bain, whose own ex-libris follows. The arms are as those of William Thomas Wishart Esquire, Representative of the ancient family of Wishart of Pitarrow, co. Forfar, recorded at Lyon Office in 1769, but seemingly used with differing crests and mottoes by various branches of the family.

Sir Hew Dalrymple of Northberwick Baronet Lord president of the session *(p. 15)*

Single coat Jacobean armorial. F.7867. Sir Hew Dalrymple (c.1652–1737) was the third son of James, 1st Viscount Stair (1619–95) and of Margaret, daughter of James Ross of Balneil, Wigtownshire. Advocate at the Scottish Bar from 1677, he became Dean of the Faculty of Advocates and Lord Advocate in 1695, Lord President of the Court of Session 1698, and was created a baronet the same year. Dalrymple was MP for New Galloway 1696–1701 and for North Berwick from 1703 until the Union in 1707. His was a notably early ex-libris in the Jacobean style.

JOHN CALLANDER of Craigforth Advocate *(p. 15)*

Single coat Chippendale armorial with supporters in a linear rectangular frame, the background shading hinting at a landscape. NIF. John Callandar (d. 1789) of Craigforth, Stirlingshire, succeeded his grandfather, of the same name and the same place. His plate was almost certainly engraved by Richard Cooper (1696/7–1764), who appears here again later. An Englishman, perhaps born in Yorkshire, he studied engraving under John Pine, travelled in Italy, and with his friend and fellow artist Alexander Guthrie visited Edinburgh, where he settled. In 1738 he married Ann Lind, youngest daughter of George Lind, merchant and baillie. He built himself a house in St John Street, and is best remembered for his portraits in line and mezzotint. See also pp. 67–68. Sir Robert Strange (see p. 58) was amongst his pupils, as was Richard's son Richard Cooper II (1740–post 1810) who studied also under Jacques Philippe Le Bas in Paris and became a painter and engraver.

Archibald Douglas *(p. 16)*

Single coat Chippendale armorial. NIF. Since the crest and motto are those of Douglas of Cavers, Roxburghshire, this probably belonged to Archibald Douglas (d. 1774),

Postmaster-General for Scotland and heritable sheriff of Teviotdale until all such heritable jurisdictions were abolished in 1745. The arms are incorrect, for the three mullets should be on a chief rather than a bar across the upper shield, and the field should be argent not or. The arms, within a bordure nebuly of the fourth, were recorded at Lyon Office in 1747 by his elder brother William, so perhaps this bookplate was engraved before then.

George Goldie Edinr, and **John Edmiston GLASGOW** *(p. 16)*

Both NIF. Two fairly typical Chippendale engraved labels, the former more precisely Scottish in its character. It is, of course, impossible to attribute them precisely, for the inscriptions contain too little information.

Robert Kennedy Esqr. of Auchtyfardel *(p. 16)*

Single coat Chippendale armorial. NIF. An advocate, he recorded these arms at Lyon Office in 1752. Auchtyfardle, the more usual spelling, is one mile north of Lesmahagow, Lanarkshire.

BOSWELLUS BOERHAAVIO PRAECEPTORI SUO *(p. 17)*

Circular portrait plate in a decorative frame, motto and festoon surrounding. Sgd: Begbie Sct Edinr. F.3136 (3137 is a reproduction). See pp. 58–60 for a note on Begbie and illustration and comment on Boswell's other bookplates.

Pringle of Clifton. HAINING LIBRARY *(p. 17)*

Single coat mantle armorial. Sgd: W. & D. Lizars sculpt. Edinr. F.24189. The Pringles of Clifton acquired parts of that barony, some ten miles south-east of Kelso in Roxburghshire, in 1619 and were known by that designation from 1686. In 1693 Andrew Pringle of Clifton recorded the arms at Lyon Office. During the latter part of the eighteenth century Mark Pringle of Fairnilee, Haining and Clifton, to which estates he had succeeded his uncle in 1790, was MP for the county of Selkirk. His son John sat in Parliament for the Selkirk district of Burghs, and on his death in 1831 was succeeded by his brother Robert, MP for Selkirk, who died unmarried. Clifton passed to his cousin Robert Elliot of Harwood, whilst the other estates went to his sister Margaret, married to Archibald Douglas. Daniel Lizars (1754–1812), the son of John Lizars, a shoemaker in Portburgh, was apprenticed to Andrew Bell, and in 1785 married Margaret, daughter of Robert Home, tailor, deceased. He worked at diverse addresses over the years, and was joined in his business by his son William Home Lizars (1788–1859), who in 1820 married Henrietta Wilson. The Lizars were prolific makers of ex-libris, and William Home was probably more widely known than any other Scottish engraver of his day. After his death his business was acquired by W. & A.K. Johnston, who continued the making of bookplates. His brother Daniel (b. 1793) worked in the family business, but went bankrupt in 1832 and emigrated to Canada the following year.

Sir Henry Hay Makdougall Bart. of Makerstoun *(p. 19)*

Quarterly spade shield festoon armorial within the ribbon of a baronet of Nova Scotia, its badge depending. F.19543. Sir Henry Hay Makdougall (*c.*1750–1825) was the only son of Lt.-Col. Sir George, 4th Bart. of the same, Roxburghshire, who assumed that surname in lieu of his patronymic of Hay (which accounts for the arms of Hay of Alderston quartering Makdougall). Sir Henry married in 1782 Isabella, second daughter of Sir James Douglas, 1st Bart. of Springwood, co. Roxburgh; and on his death without sons the baronetcy passed to his cousin Thomas Hay, while Makerstoun went to his eldest daughter Anna Maria, Lady Brisbane. The Makdougall or Makdougal arms were granted by patent in 1698 and registered at Lyon Office in 1741. This ancient family descended from Fergus, granted the lands of Makerstoun by Robert II in 1374, and was probably a branch of the Galloway MacDowells.

James Boyd, LL.D *(p. 19)*

Crest, with helm and mantling. Sgd: J & J Johnstone sc. F.3365. An example of a stock pattern design, it was used also by Colin Campbell and A. Maclean, *et al.* James Boyd (1795–1856) was educated at Glasgow University, of which he became an MA. He was House Governor at George Heriot's Hospital, Edinburgh 1825–9, and in the former year an honorary LL.D was conferred on him by his old university. In 1829 he was appointed classical master at Edinburgh High School, a post he held until his death. Boyd was for many years secretary to the Society of Edinburgh Teachers, and, after his death an award, known as the Boyd Medal, was instituted in his memory for pupils at the school. James and John Johnstone were engravers and copperplate printers in Edinburgh 1790–1830, but only a small number of bookplates bear their signature.

James Johnston, or Johnstone, married Charlotte, daughter of writer Lauchlan Grant, in 1791. He was at Warrington's Close 1793–7, Stamp Office Close 1799, and at 396 Castlehill in 1832. He and John (d. 1860), plates by whom are illustrated in Vol. 2 of Dibden's *Biographical Tour*, 1838 were together at 134 High Street 1825–8 and then at 20 North Bridge.

Dr. Paterson. 32 Charlotte Street, LEITH *(p. 19)*

Pictorial showing books on a ledge, and a scroll, within a decorative oval frame incorporating leaves and flowers. Sgd: Scott & Ferguson Sct. Like the above, a favoured stock pattern. Others who opted for it included John Dunn, Hugh Elder and Peter Samuel. Alexander Scott, engraver and lithographer in Edinburgh, acquired the business of James Kirkwood & Son in 1850 at South St Andrew's Street, and two years later he was joined by Ferguson at the same address, where they remained until 1859. Finally, until 1895, they were in Clyde Street, but Morrison & Gibb absorbed the firm *c.*1896. Some half dozen other ex-libris bear their signature.

HAROLD NELSON HIS BOOK OF BOOK-PLATES *(p. 21)*

Title-page design, 1904. Schulze and his publications are recorded in the introduction. This particular book was published in an edition of 325 copies, 25 of them on Japanese vellum and numbered and signed by the artist.

EX LIBRIS WILLIAM GILCHRIST MACBETH *(p. 23)*

Armorial within a Celtic decorative frame. Unsigned, but the work of Graham Johnston (see p. 26). William Gilchrist Macbeth (1887–1948), JP, of Dunira, Perthshire, was the only son of George Alexander Macbeth (1844–1919), JP, shipowner of Glasgow, and of his wife Mary Reid. He recorded the arms at Lyon Office in 1919. Macbeth created elaborate terraced gardens at Dunira to the designs of Thomas H. Mawson.

Ex Libris AGNES DUNLOP *(p. 23)*

Wood-engraved pictorial by William McLaren (b. 1923), of Hamilton, Lanarkshire, who studied under Joan Hassall at the Edinburgh College of Art 1940–6. In addition to bookjackets and illustrations (notably for Beverley Nichols' books) he made hundreds of drawings for *Radio Times*; and in addition to portraits and landscapes has painted murals for such as Hopetoun House, Tyninghame in East Lothian and Wemyss Castle in Fife. Though he has made few ex-libris, they span decades. Agnes Dunlop, the novelist Elizabeth Kyle, is referred to in the introduction. His bookplate for Lady Mary Russell follows (pp. 130–131).

KATHLEEN FINLAY HORSMAN *(p. 23)*

Pictorial. The composition of this and its printing have already been referred to. Joan Hassall engraved the plate on wood, planning for printing in black, grey-blue, red and yellow. Miss Horsman was an Edinburgh friend, and details of her are elusive, but she was referred to in a letter from the engraver to her brother and sister-in-law in March 1946. It, and images of the ex-libris in colour and black alone are on pp. 135–6 of *Dearest Joana A selection of Joan Hassall's life-time letters and art*, edited by Brian North Lee, Fleece Press, Wakefield, 2000. Joan Hassall (1906–88), wood engraver, book illustrator and painter, produced 35 bookplates. See David Chambers, *Joan Hassall Engravings & Drawings*, 1985.

James Curle Priorwood Melrose
(Back cover illustration)

Etched pictorial showing the south transept of Melrose Abbey, the work of Sir David Young Cameron (see p. 20), 1911. James Curle (1862–1944), eldest son of Alexander Curle and Christian, only daughter of Sir James Anderson, married in 1902 Alice Mary Blanchette, only daughter of Colonel Herbert A. T. Nepean, of the Indian Staff Corps. A writer to the signet, and FSA, he was a member of the Archaeological Institute of the German Empire, and a member of the Royal Commission on Ancient Monuments for Scotland, etc. The excavation of the Roman fort, Trimontium, at Newstead near Melrose, 1905–10, was directed by him. Melrose Abbey was founded in 1136 by King David I, but was badly damaged by the English in 1385 and 1544. Its preservation more recently depended on money supplied by the 5th Duke of Buccleuch and energy expended by Sir Walter Scott in 1822.

Notes on the text

Since the ex-libris which principally feature here are all illustrated, it seemed unnecessary to detail in general arms or other components, for they are there for the reader's scrutiny; but an exception was made if and when there was something of especial interest to be said. This economy allowed fuller biographical or other detailing of worth. Examples mentioned in passing are also necessarily summarily referred to, but the owner and artist index at the end of the book should enable easy reference. Inscriptions are given in full, in upper or lower case as used, but dots or ornaments which occasionally feature between words are ignored. Where inscriptional references to places are archaic or otherwise differ from those familiar now, the current spellings follow in the text. The same applies to surnames. Signatures of makers and years of making are cited if they occur, and in the case of engravers or artists represented by more than one work there is a note on them generally at their first appearance. Virtually all the abbreviations in the text are standard and familiar, but for readers who are not bookplate collectors it should be explained that "NIF" indicates that the ex-libris under discussion is not in the great Sir Augustus Wollaston Franks Collection at the British Museum, and "F" followed by a number indicates inclusion therein. "V" signifies that a plate is in the George Heath Viner Collection which is complementary to Franks and alongside it in the Print Room. Although the placing of illustrations is very loosely chronological, exceptions were made wherever appropriate in order to show types or styles of bookplates together in comfortable juxtaposition. "Fincham" indicates Henry W. Fincham's *Artists and Engravers of British and American Book Plates*, published by Kegan Paul, Trench, Trubner & Co. Ltd. London 1897. Though often sadly inaccurate in precise detail, it remains the classic text on the subject since it has not been superseded. George Herbert Bushnell's *Scottish Engravers,* Oxford University Press, 1949, was likewise a valuable and obvious source of information, and has been drawn upon markedly. Its only weakness is that Bushnell accepted Fincham's suggested dates for bookplates too literally, for they were in fact mere guesstimates, and often somewhat wide of the mark from other evidences. Extensive additions to Bushnell can be found online at the *Scottish Book Trades Index* website at www.nls.uk/catalogues/resources/sbti . Numerous other sources are cited in the text.

SCOTTISH
BOOKPLATES

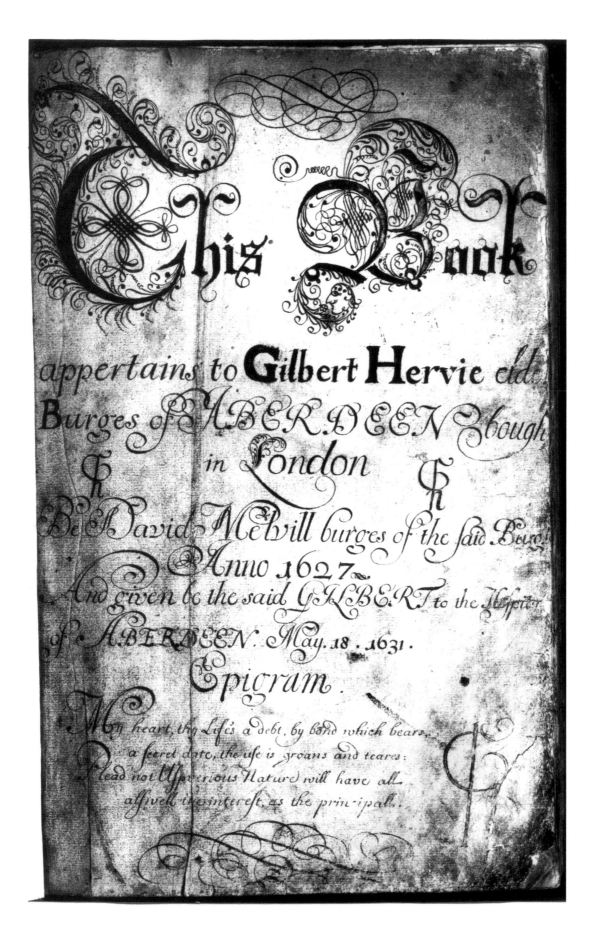

This Book

appertains to **Gilbert Hervie** elder

Burges of ABERDEEN bough

in London

Be David Melvill burges of the said Burg

Anno 1627

And given be the said GILBERT to the Hospitl

of ABERDEEN. May. 18 . 1631.

Epigram.

My heart, thy Life's a debt, by bond which bears
a seerd date, the use is groans and teares:
Plead not Usureous Nature will have all
alsweill the interest, as the prin-ipall.

Scottish Bookplates

This Book appertains to Gilbert Hervie elder Burgess of ABERDEEN bought in London Be David Melvill burges of the said Burgh Anno 1627 And given be the said GILBERT to the Hospitall of ABERDEEN. May. 18. 1631. (An epigram follows).

An elaborate and beautifully ornamented inscription in a copy of a folio *Bible*, printed by Robert Barker, London, 1617. Also within the same, pasted at different places on the leaves of the book is a printed label, 8 × 3cm, which reads: This Bible is given to the Hospitall of ABERDENE, by Gilbert Hervie, elder, Burges of the sayd BURGH, May 18,1631. It seemed here, however, more pertinent to show the manuscript inscription, which as you see goes so far as to say where the Bible was purchased and by whom. Edward Raban, who printed the label, was – as already stated on p. 8 – an Englishman of German descent, and was most probably connected with the family of Raben, printers of Frankfurt. He was in Edinburgh by 1620, but the same year moved to St. Andrews, where he set up his press (at the sign of "A.B.C" in the South Street), but in 1622 moved north again to Aberdeen, and remained at "The Townes Armes" upon the Market Place for the rest of his career, though from 1643 he also had a shop in the Broad Gate. He in 1662 became printer to the University and the Town. Gilbert Hervie of Elrick was the son of James Hervye, advocate, and died in 1656. David Melvill is also easily identified, for he was surely the Aberdeen book-seller for whom Raban printed many of his upwards of 150 books. The *Bible* is now preserved in Aberdeen Town House, and for a fuller account of it see *The Toun's Great Bible*, by J.P. Edmond, privately printed, Aberdeen, 1885. Though it is necessary here to concentrate on printed ex-libris, there were manuscript examples over centuries, in Scotland and England, some of them very well executed, and they take their part as evidences of bibliophily. Indeed, two Aberdeen examples in the Lee Collection were made 200 years after the illustration here. One is inscribed JANE GORDON Dee Street Aberdeen, and the other Keith Gordon Aberdeen 13 December 1823 (below).

JOHN ABERNETHIE of Mayen, August 1. 1691

Printed label, the inscription below a row of horizontal ornaments. Note the naivety of the arrangements of the ornaments which include two question marks, one inverted. NIF. V.17. There is a volume of 1695, but without title, place, date or imprint, entitled *Additional information for John Abernethie of Mayen against Sir John Gordon of Park, and his cedent.* and an Act of Parliament (in a volume of such Acts published 1695), *Act and remit the Laird of Rothiemay. and Abernethy of Mayens.* See Johnstone and Robertson. *Bibliographia Aberdonensis*, Aberdeen, 1929. This Mayen family descended from Alexander Abernethy of Wester Saltoun, second son of Alexander, 6th Lord Abernethy of Saltoun.

The Right Honble Sr Alexr. Campbell of Cesnok one of the Senators of the Colledge of Justice and one of the Lords of Her Maties most Honble Privy Counsell & Exchequer &c: 1707

Early armorial: 1. Campbell, 2 & 3 Hume quartering Polwarth, Sinclair and Pepdie of Dunglass, 4 Campbell of Loudoun; two mottoes, the inscription on a mantle at base. NIF. It seems of Scottish engraving. Sir Alexander Campbell of Cesnok (1675–1740) assumed the surname in lieu of Hume following his marriage to Margaret, second daughter and eventually heir of Sir George Campbell of Cessnock, Ayrshire (d.1704). He was the third son of Sir Patrick Hume of Redbraes, Berwickshire (1641–1724), created Earl of Marchmont in 1696, whose ex-libris follows. An advocate at the Scottish Bar, knighted in 1696, he sat in the Scottish Parliament for Kirkwall 1698–1702 and for Berwickshire 1706–7, was a Lord of Session as Lord Cessnock 1704–14, when he resigned, and was a Privy Councillor and Lord of the Exchequer. On the death of his elder and childless brother Patrick in 1709 he assumed the courtesy title of Lord Polwarth and resumed the surname of Hume. Ambassador to Denmark 1715–21 and appointed Lord Clerk Register 1716, in 1722 he became First Ambassador to the Congress of Cambria, remaining in that post until 1725, in which year he succeeded his father as 2nd Earl of Marchmont. As Lord Polwarth he had other bookplates, dated 1721 and 1722, and two as Earl of Marchmont, both dated 1725.

(Preston, Baronet)

Anonymous single coat early armorial, the badge of a baronet of Nova Scotia at mid point, with supporters, etc. F.24097. The Franks Catalogue calls it a Jacobean armorial and ascribes it to the 4th Baronet, who succeeded in 1741, and was surely wrong on both counts. It almost certainly belonged to Sir William Preston (d.1702–5), first son and heir of "Master George Preston fear of Valafield" (i.e. heir to Valleyfield), who was created baronet in 1637. He married Anne, daughter of Sir James Lumsden of Invergelly. The bookplate may well have been also used by Sir George, the 3rd Bart. (c.1670–1741), who married Agnes, daughter of Patrick Muirhead, of Rashyhill, a lady famed for her beauty.

The Right Honorable Thomas Lord Viscount Dupplin, Lord Balhousie. 1699

Single coat early armorial, engraved in the London workshop of William Jackson. F.14194 & *567. Thomas Hay (d.1719) of Balhousie, Perthshire, second but eldest surviving son of George Hay of the same (d.1672) descended from Peter Hay, a younger brother of George, 1st Earl of Kinnoull. MP for the County of Perth 1693–7, he was created 1697 Viscount Dupplin and Lord Balhousie, took his seat the next year, and became a commissioner for the Union. He succeeded his cousin as 8th Earl of Kinnoull in 1709. There seems no reason to suppose he intended joining the 1715 rising, but he was suspected of Jacobite sympathies and imprisoned for a time in Edinburgh Castle. He married in 1683 Margaret (or Elizabeth), daughter of William Drummond, 1st Viscount Strathallan. His spirited supporters and crest depict Lowland Scots countrymen.

The Achivement of the Rigt. Honoble Sir Robert Blackwood of Pittrevie Lod Provest of Edinburgh

Single coat armorial, the crest of which seems to be upside down, and an instance of the curious inscriptional abbreviations found on some early eighteenth century Scottish armorials. Sgd: Ard. Burdon (sic) Sculp. NIF. An excessively rare plate by Archibald Burden (for comment on whom see pp. 10 and 27) not engraved for Nisbet's *System of Heraldry* and assuredly an ex-libris. In that work, however, the Blackwood arms are referred to as appearing in Workman's MS, which belonged to James Workman, herald painter in the reign of James VI, and which is now in Lyon Office. This refers to Henry and Adam Blackwood.

JOHN ABERNETHIE of *Mayen*,
Auguſt 1. 1691.

UT
CRESCAM PROSIM

CONSTANTER ET PRUDENTER

The Right Honble Sr Alexr Campbell
of Cesnok one of the Senators of the
Colledge of Justice and one of the Lords of
Her Maties most Honble Privy Counsell & Exchequer
&c: 1707

PRÆSTO UT PRÆSTEM

RENOVATE ANIMOS.

The Right Honorable Thomas Lord Viscount
Dupplin, Lord Balhousie .1699.

PER VIAS RECTAS

The Atchivement of the Rigt Hono^ble
Sir Robert Blackwood of Pittrevie
Lo^d Provest of Edinburgh

Ar^d Burdon ────────────── Sculp

A DEO LUMEN

Lord Charles Kerr Director of
his Majestys Chancellary

NOBILIS IRA

AVITO VIRET HONORE

James Earle of Bute &c.
GEO PATERSON SCULP

SUFFER SUFFER

The Honble John Haldane of
Gleneagles 1707

38

Robert Blackwood, when "Dean of Gild of the town of Edinburgh", recorded arms at Lyon Office, "Argent a saltyre sable on a chief of the second three oak leaves proper, a mascle gules for difference, with crest rays or beams of the sun proper and motto "Per vias rectas" (Vol. 1, p. 258 1704–5). The mascle does not appear on the bookplate, which probably means that it was made before the matriculation of arms. Sir Robert was Dean of Guild before becoming Lord Provost. He bought Pitreavie from the Wardlaws *c.*1713, and it remained in the Blackwood family until the latter nineteenth century.

Lord Charles Kerr Director of his Majestys Chancellary

Single coat armorial. F.17076. Lord Charles Kerr (d. 1736) was the second son of Robert, Earl of Ancrum and 1st Marquess of Lothian and of Lady Jean Campbell, daughter of Archibald, 1st and last Marquess of Argyll. He was appointed Director of Chancery in 1703, which appointment was renewed in 1722 to him and to his son Robert "during their joint lives". In 1707 he bought the estate of Kings Cramond near Edinburgh, but sold it again in 1718. He married in 1684 Janet, elder daughter of Sir David Murray of Stanhope, Bt. and of Lady Anne Bruce, second daughter of Alexander, 2nd Earl of Kincardine, who gave him 14 children and died 1755.

James Stuart Earle of Bute &c.

Single coat armorial with supporters, etc. Sgd: GEO. PATERSON SCULP. F.28440. George Paterson(e), engraver in Edinburgh, subscribed to Nisbet's *Essay on … Armories*, 1718, but details of his career are elusive. James Stuart, 2nd Earl of Bute, who succeeded his father in 1710, was the only son of James, 1st Earl, created 1703, and of Agnes, eldest daughter of Sir George Mackenzie of Rosehaugh, Ross-shire (1636–91), "Bloody Mackenzie" to the Covenanters, who was appointed King's Advocate in 1677. After the death of his maternal uncle, George Mackenzie of Rosehaugh, and following considerable litigation, he succeeded to sizeable estates. A Lord of the Bedchamber from 1721, he married in 1711 Lady Anne Campbell, daughter of Archibald, 1st Duke of Argyll, who, as his widow, married in 1731 Alexander Fraser of Strichen, and died 1736.

The Honble. John Haldane of Gleneagles 1707

Early armorial (Haldane quartering Lennox and Menteith, tinctured wrongly), from the London workshop of William Jackson. F.13240. John Haldane (1660–1721), 14th Laird of Gleneagles, Perthshire, was a captain in the Earl of Perth's Horse 1685, commissioner for the county in the convention of 1687, and member for Perthshire in the last Scottish Parliament 1705–8, in which he strongly supported the ill-fated Darien adventure. On the Government's side in the 1715 Jacobite rising he suffered much damage to his property at the hands of the rebels. The family, at Gleneagles from the fourteenth century, descend from the Haldanes of that Ilk first recorded in a charter from King William the Lion.

George Lockhart of Carnwath

Single coat armorial, also from William Jackson's workshop. F.18566. George Lockhart (1676–1732), 2nd Laird of Carnwath, Lanark, was MP for the shire of Edinburgh from 1703 to the union in 1707. Though not personally "out" in 1715, he was strongly Jacobite, and was in effect the Old Pretender's chief undercover agent in Scotland until in 1717 his correspondence was intercepted and he fled to Holland. On George I's death he was allowed back to Scotland. By his wife Lady Euphemia Montgomerie, daughter of Alexander, 9th Earl of Eglinton, he had 14 surviving children. Only son of Sir George, of Carstairs, and grandson of Sir James, 12th Laird of Lee, Lanarkshire, he directly descended in the male line from Philip Locard

CORDA SERATA FERO

George Lockhart of Carnwath

who acquired the lands of Lee *c.*1272. The bookplate predates his matriculation at Lyon Office in 1730, when a bordure azure charged with five mullets argent was added to his arms. A smaller version of his bookplate is F.18567.

John McDowall of Logan LR

Single coat armorial of Scottish engraving. F.19182. John MacDowall, or McDouall (d.1754), 10th Laird of Logan, Wigtonshire, was eldest son of Robert McDowall of Logan (d.*c.*1729), and descended from Dougal Mcdouall (d by 1414) who renounced his Logan lands to Archibald, 4th Earl of Douglas, who re-granted them to Thomas McDouall, his son and heir.

The Right Honble. Patrick Hume Earl of Marchmont Viscount of Blasonberry Lord Polwarth of Polwarth &c Lord High Chancelor of Scotland 1702

Quarterly armorial from William Jackson's workshop. F.15696. Sir Patrick Hume (1641–1724), 1st Earl of Marchmont, created Baron Polwarth 1690, became Chancellor of Scotland in 1696 and Earl and Viscount, etc. in 1697. In 1660 he married Grisell, daughter of Sir Thomas Kerr of Cavers, Roxburghshire. Eldest son of Sir Patrick

Hume of Polwarth, Bart. (d.1648), he became MP for Berwickshire, but due to constant opposition to the Duke of Lauderdale's policies he was summoned by the council in 1675, declared "a factious person…incapable of all public trust", and imprisoned. Released 1676 by order of the King he went abroad. He and other dissident Scottish noblemen first thought of buying New York for £15,000, but then preferred founding a settlement in Carolina. Suspected next of involvement in the Rye House Plot, Patrick was attainted and his estates sequestrated. He hid in the vault of Polwarth Church, where his daughter Grisell fed him, then under the floor of Redbraes House. It was too damp, so he fled to London and then to Holland and the protection of the Prince of Orange, whose great friend he became. Joined by his wife and nine children, he lived in Utrecht until his return to Scotland to join the Earl of Argyll's rising. It failed, so he hid again, escaped to Bordeaux, and then in Utrecht practised as a surgeon until his return to England with William of Orange, whereupon his estates were restored. His armorial shows 1 & 4 Hume quartering Pepdie, Polwarth and Sinclair, with at mid point on an escutcheon a crowned orange, the augmentation of honour granted by William III when he was raised to the Earldom and became Chancellor of Scotland. Note, too, the oranges above the lower motto scroll.

Judge Nott

Fax Mentis Honesta Gloria

(Areskine or Erskine)

Anonymous Early Armorial. NIF. This extremely rare armorial has been the subject of debate both as to its engraver and the family of its owner. George Heath Viner was of the opinion that it was the work of David Loggan (*c.*1630–93), who was born at Dantzic, came to England before the Restoration, and is best remembered for his engravings of Oxford and Cambridge. Viner wrote an article on ex-libris which were perhaps by Loggan, but it was unpublished during his lifetime and eventually appeared in *The Bookplate Society Newsletter* for October 1973. Of the nine he recorded, he concluded that the Ent and Freke plates were by other hands, and was certainly absolutely right about the Sir George Ent's armorial, for it was in use when Loggan was but a young man, years before he became to Britain. The first thing which strikes one about the plate shown here is the quality of its mantling, and the model(s) for it came to Viner's eye by serendipity. He happened one day to be glancing at the illustrations in Dr. Strohl's *Heraldischer Atlas*, and found a page illustrating some fifteen facsimile reproductions of early mantled shields with helms. The ones of particular interest – 11 to 15 – were attributed to Michel le Blon (*c*.1590–1656). They were also, incidentally, to be illustrated in Fox-Davies' *The Art of Heraldry*, on page CIX. The Erskine is a combination of Le Blon Nos.11 & 13, and with the exception of the top curvings of the mantling is wholly after No. 13. As you will notice, the helm is diapered, the motto scroll is split and has globular ends, and the script lettering of the two Isham ex-libris which Loggan engraved (the correspondence in respect of which survives) is repeated. It is also worthy of note that the motto "Fax mentis honestae gloria", not apparently a customary one with the Erskine family, occurs also on the Humberston armorial which was almost certainly from Loggan's graver. This armorial is thus one of perhaps only two by Loggan which can firmly be attributed to the seventeenth century. Whether Loggan met Erskine in London, Oxford or Cambridge we can but surmise, but it was almost certainly one of them for he is not recorded as having visited Scotland. By 1675 he was living in Leicester Fields, and he let his lodgings to persons of quality.

The bookplate was No.270 for identification in *The Ex-Libris Journal*, Vol. 8, 1899, facing p. 12, and two correspondents wrote expressing their views. Mrs. A. Stuart wrote: "One of the Erskines of Dun. Nisbet, in his *System of Heraldry*, says: Argent, on a pale sable, a sword of the first, point downward, for the surname of Dun, upon the account that Sir Robert Erskine of that Ilk … married the heiress of Dun of that Ilk, who carried Gules, a sword in pale argent: their younger son, in obtaining his mother's inheritance, placed the sword upon the pale of Erskine, for his difference from the principal family. Some of the old books of painting represent the sword as a cross croslet fitched or, taking it to be one of these in the earldom of Mar". F. J. Thairlwall wrote at even greater length: "I believe (it) to be Areskin or Erskine, though I fear the evidence I have of this will not be considered as enough for identification. The general coat of Erskine is Arg., a pale sa. But many branches bear the pale charged. For instance, Areskine Scotland, Arg., on a pale sa. a cross patty fitchy of the first (Papworth, p. 1005); Erskine, Sheefield, co. Roxburgh, Arg., on a pale sa. a cross crosslet fitchy or, a bord. az. (Burke's 'Armory', last edition, p. 329); Erskine, Pittodrie, Aberdun, Ar., on a pale sa. 3 fleurs-de-lis or (same place); and so on. The first two examples I have given come

very close to No. 270. Then the crest is also that of Erskine, A hand holding a club, with motto, 'Judge nought'. For instance, Erskine, Scotland, In a dexter hand a club, raguly ppr., 'Judge nought' (Fairbairn, p. 171); Thomas Erskine of Linlathen, the same crest and motto (same place); James Erskine, "A dexter hand holding a baton ppr., 'Judge nought' (Burke's 'Armory', p. 329); Erskine Earl of Buchan, A dexter arm holding a club or baton raguled proper, 'Judge not' (same page). These come very near A dexter cubit arm holding a baton or mace, ppr., and motto, 'Judge Nott". So, for what it is worth, I submit this suggested identification for consideration". How one wishes the bookplate had borne its owner's name, place of residence, and a date; but it is surely Erskine (however spelt), and the cross-crosslet derives from Mar.

The Right Honble. Robert Lord Viscount of Arbuthnott

Early armorial, engraved in the London workshop of William Jackson. F.653 & *502. Robert Arbuthnott (1686–1710), 4th Viscount, succeeded his father in 1694. In 1706, soon after reaching his majority, he left Scotland and appeared with "an equipage suiting his quality" at the court of England. After travelling throughout Holland and part of Germany he returned to London until he was advised to go to Bath by his physicians. He died there, and was succeeded by his brother John, who used a Jacobean armorial bookplate (F.652).

Sr. John Anstruther of that ilk Baronet

Early armorial, engraved in the London workshop of
William Jackson. F.615 & *518. Sir John Anstruther of
Anstruther, Fife (1678–1753) was the only son of Sir
William Anstruther, Kt. (d.1711), and was created baronet
in 1700. He married at Edinburgh in 1717 Lady Mary
Carmichael, eldest daughter of James, 2nd Earl of
Hyndford, by Elizabeth his wife, daughter of John
Maitland, Earl of Lauderdale. He died at Elie House, co.
Fife. The Anstruthers had been seated in Fife since at least
1100 and are descended in the direct male line from William
de Candela, Lord of Anstruthers who flourished in the
reign of King David. Sir William, above, was unusual in
that he was one of five brothers who were all knighted.
Through Sir John's marriage their descendants succeeded
to the Carmichael estates in Lanarkshire and elsewhere on
the death of the last Earl of Hyndford in 1817.

The Achievement of John Earle of Wigtonn Lord
fleming

Early Scottish armorial (Fleming quartering Hamilton).
F.10748. John Fleming (c.1673–1744), 6th Earl of Wigtown
and 11th Lord Fleming, followed the Old Pretender into
exile and was sent to seminaries abroad where it is thought
he became a Roman Catholic. He succeeded his father in
1681. Returning to Scotland he sat in the parliament of
1706, opposing the Treaty of Union, and at the outbreak of
the Jacobite rising of 1715 he was imprisoned in Edinburgh
Castle as a suspect, at which he protested strongly. It was
almost a year before he was released. He was appointed
King's Chamberlain of Fife in 1736. Fleming had married in
1698 Lady Margaret Lindsay, daughter of the 3rd Earl of
Balcarres, but he divorced her in 1708 for adultery with
Lord Belhaven. In 1711 he married secondly Lady Mary
Keith, daughter of the 19th Earl Marischel; and after her
death in 1721 he married Eupheme, daughter of George
Lockhart of Carnwath, who survived him.

Erskine of Dun

Quarterly coat Jacobean armorial (Erskine quartering Dun of that Ilk). Sgd: A Burden S. NIF. Although only the third son of his father, he inherited the lands of Dun, his two elder brothers John and James having been disinherited, one for marrying against his father's wishes, the other for taking part in the Jacobite rising of 1715. He sat in the Scottish parliament of 1690 to 1699 and opposed the Union; and he was a Lord of Session, as Lord Dun, from 1710 to 1753. These last two bookplates indicate the concurrent character of Scottish early armorial and Jacobean compositions. Notice the inferior lettering, already commented on, and its inharmonious placing.

Chas. Bruce Glasier in Edinburgh. MDCCX

Crest and inscription within an ambitious architectural frame. F.4142. The crest is that of the large "clan" of Bruces descended from Sir Robert de Bruys of Clackmannan (d. c.1390), who received from King David – son of Robert the Bruce – the estate and manor of Clackmannan in 1359. It included the Bruces of Kennet, perhaps the senior line, of Airth, of Kinnaird, of Stenhouse, and others, some using an arm "embowed", others upright, all holding a sceptre and most with the motto "Fuimus". It does nothing but indicate descent from the Clakmannan Bruces, who are legion. One has but to study such as eighteenth century Scottish gravestones to see crests and arms marking the resting places of folk of apparently modest employment, for in a small country like Scotland the boast may well have been literally true. Everyone was related to everyone else.

Birnie of Broomhill

Jacobean armorial-pictorial with ministers at their desks as supporters. Sgd: Ar(chibal)d Burden Sculp. (He has already been commented on). The original copper (F.2612) was reworked (F.2613) to depict the ministers in longer gowns, but it survived in good condition and there were re-strikes in the late nineteenth century. This ex-libris presumably belonged to Alexander Birnie (1707–62) of Broomhill, Lanarkshire, who married Margaret Weir. Broomhill had been a Hamilton property. The Rev. James Hamilton, who became bishop of Galloway in 1661, owned it, and his daughter and eventual heiress Jean married John Birnie. The estate remained in that family until sold about 1825. The arms were recorded at Lyon Office in 1698.

THE ARMORIAL BEARINGS OF MR. JOHN BALVAIRD. M.D.

An exceedingly rare armorial (NIF; Hall Crouch Collection). Its ownerhip is in no doubt, for the arms were granted by Lyon Office 1672–4 to "Mr John Balvaird M.D", who was chaplain to the Archbishop of St Andrews, albeit with the motto Non omnius dormio – not that that signifies, for they were changeable at will regardless of what a King of Arms approved. Stylistically comparable examples are elusive, but it is quite possible that this is our earliest extant Scottish bookplate *per se* insofar as had it served dual-purpose as a cut for an armory it would have been less modest.

William Cuming M:D

Jacobean armorial, with busts in the four comers within the rectangular frame. NIF. William Cuming (1714–88), MD of Rheims, MD of Edinburgh 1752, lived at Dorchester, Dorset. The busts are Hippocrates, Sydenham, Boerhaave, and John Freind. Though the arms shown on his bookplate are not recorded at Lyon Office, they could well have been, for they are a perfectly reasonably differenced version of Cuming. In the Scottish tradition a bordure charged with eight roses, and by what seems to be a fleur-de-lys on a mullet, indicate the fifth son of a third son. The crest, moreover, hints at a medical man interested in astral manifestations; and the "insignia" around the arms, with stars and interlocked hands, suggests that he belonged to an association of like-minded scholars. If the hypothesis is correct, the arms, busts, crest and other accoutrements add up to a mini-biography.

Sir Charles Gilmour of Craigmiller Bart.

Single coat Jacobean armorial in an oval frame. F.11953. Sir Charles Gilmour of Craigmillar, Midlothian, 2nd Bart. was the eldest son of Sir Alexander Gilmour (1651–1731), who was created a baronet of Nova Scotia in 1678 and married Grizel, daughter of George, 11th Lord Ross of Hallhead. Sir Charles (d.1751) was MP for Edinburgh 1737–47, Paymaster of the Board of Works 1742, and Commissioner for Trade and Plantation 1747. He married in 1733 Jean, daughter of Sir Robert Sinclair of Longformacus, Berwickshire, 3rd Bart. Sir Charles recorded these arms at Lyon Office in 1733 in lieu of those recorded 1672–7 by his grandfather, Sir George Gilmour.

William Nisbet of Dirleton Esqr.

Single coat Jacobean armorial in an oval frame. F.21907. He used, however, another probably very similar plate which was noted in the Marshall sale catalogue of 1906 (lot 677). An early armorial composition for Nisbet of Dirleton (F.21900) was probably not a bookplate. The Nisbets of Dirleton, East Lothian, descended from Henry Nisbet, Provost of Edinburgh 1597–8, whose son Sir John (1610–88), Lord Advocate and a Lord of Session 1664–7 bought the Dirleton estate in 1663. He recorded arms at Lyon Office in 1672. Though married three times he had no male heir and bequeathed his estate to a kinsman, William, son of Alexander Nisbet of Craigintinnie (b.1666). He was the first of a line of three Williams of Dirleton, his son being William (d.1733). The grandson William (d.1783), married Mary, only child and heiress of Alexander Hamilton of Pencaitland and Dechmont and heiress of entail of John, 5th Lord Belhaven.

William Scott Advocate

Single coat Jacobean armorial in an oval frame. F.26323. These arms are not apparently recorded at Lyon Office, and are seemingly a differenced version of Scott of Ancrum with alternative crest and motto.

Orr of Barrowfield

Single coat Jacobean armorial in a cartouche which incorporates cornucopiae at left and right in reference to the family's crest. F.22413. This must date from post-1730 when John Orr acquired the estate of Barrowfield, then about two miles south-east of the city, from the magistrates of the City of Glasgow, by whom it had been compulsorily purchased from John Walkinshaw due to the part he played in the Jacobite rising of 1715 and his subsequent imprisonment. John Orr, a merchant in Glasgow, whose forbears came from Cambusnethan in Lanarkshire, recorded these arms at Lyon Office in 1731. Barrowfield was sold in 1788 to the Hoziers of Newlands, the next door estate.

(Maitland, Earl of Lauderdale)

Anonymous single coat oval woodcut armorial, dated "ANNO 1716" on the same ribbon as the motto "CONSILIO ET ANIMIS". F.19495 (F.19496, also a woodcut, shows the escutcheon and coronet on a single supporter) and both are within wreaths. Arms: Or a lion rampant dechaussé gules within a double tressure flory counterflory azure. Charles Maitland (1688–1744), 6th Earl of Lauderdale, succeeded his father in 1710, and fought as an officer at the battle of Sheriffmuir in 1715. He was Captain-General of the Mint, Praeses of the Board of Police and Lord Lieutenant and Sheriff Principal of the county of Edinburgh. In 1741 he was elected a representative peer for Scotland. He married in 1710 Lady Elizabeth Ogilvy, daughter of James, 4th Earl of Findlater and 1st Earl of Seafield, who died at Bath 1778. Their eldest surviving son, James, succeeded.

The Honble George Baillie Esqr. one of the Lords of the Treasury. 1724

Single coat Jacobean armorial. Sgd: R: Cooper Sculp. F.1163. The virtually identical larger one is sgd: A Johnston Sculp (F.1162), but another state (v.163) lacks the date. It is curious that two similar plates identically worded for the same man should have different engravers, but a reasonable explanation is that Cooper was in 1724 Johnston's pupil, entrusted to produce the smaller version. Andrew Johnston (c.1700–50) was a Scottish engraver, probably in Edinburgh, who produced maps for Camden's *Britannia*, etc. His ex-libris for Robert Hunter follows. As mentioned on p.28, Richard Cooper senior studied engraving under John Pine – perhaps after a spell with Johnston. The Hon. George Baillie (d.1738) was the son of Robert Baillie of Jerviswoode (c.1634–84), executed for his alleged complicity in the Rye House Plot against Charles II. Robert was held in the Tolbooth in Edinburgh for ten months and submitted to appalling torture (he was, interestingly, a great-grandson of John Knox). George fled penniless after his father's death and joined Patrick Hume, later Earl of Marchmont (his bookplate has already been shown), whose heroic young daughter Grisell he already knew. They fell in love and married in 1691. Hume and Baillie returned to England with William III, and Baillie became an MP and an architect of the Treaty of Union. He built Mellerstain, designed by William Adam (it is depicted in the Lady Mary Russell ex-libris which follows). Grissell was, however, the "star" of the house's story, and her "Household Book" has become a classic of social history. Baillie's library mostly survives, and many of his books have his device of a golden fleece on their spines, in addition to ex-libris inside.

Thomas Calderwood of POLTON Esq.

Single coat Jacobean armorial, probably of English engraving. NIF. Polton is near Lasswade in Midlothian. Thomas, who must have owned the bookplate, recorded arms at Lyon Office in 1736, and the ex-libris probably dates from the same period. He was surely the son of Sir William Calderwod of Polton (1661–1733), advocate 1687, deputy sheriff of the County of Edinburgh, who was knighted c.1707. Lord of Session 1711 with the title of Lord Polton, he was grandson of Alexander Calderwood, bailie of Dalkeith, and nephew of Dr William Calderwood, minister there and great-nephew of the Rev. David Calderwood (1575–1650), the ecclesiastical historian. The latter gained fame, or notoriety, by arguing with King James VI & I in 1617 against the decree giving power to direct the external policy of the Church of Scotland to the king and the bishops, which led to his being deprived of his charge at Dalkeith, imprisoned, and then exiled, returning on the death of the king in 1625. He was author of The *History of the Kirk of Scotland*, eight volumes, 1642–9. Thomas of the bookplate married Margaret (1717–74), daughter of Sir James Steuart of Coltness, Bart. They had two sons and a daughter, and the daughter eventually inherited Polton.

Thomas Calderwood of POLTON Esq.

Anonymous

A strange little composition within a Jacobean cartouche, which appears to have been made as a bookplate. NIF. The Robertsons of Lude, Perthshire, have a sleeping dog for crest and use as a motto "Dinna waken sleeping dogs". Here a decidedly somnolent spaniel (who doesn't look as if he would harm anyone even when awake) lies at the foot of a thistle growing upon a mound. "BOURDNAE" means "Don't touch, or meddle with", and "WAKENAE" is self-evident. Perhaps it all just signifies: "Do not deride the prickle lest it prick you nor wake not the dog lest he bite you", a pleasant conceit of a warning kind.

His Excellency Robert Hunter Esqr Captain General & Chief Governour of Jamaica

Jacobean single coat armorial. F.15778. Sgd: A. Johnston, and thus engraved by Andrew Johnston, who was certainly Scottish and probably worked in Edinburgh, c.1700–50. He engraved maps of Scotland for the 1722 edition of Camden's *Britannia*, and several mezzotint portraits, three of which bear London addresses. Eight ex-libris signed by him are recorded. A second state of the Hunter ex-libris (NIF) has the motto ARTE NON IMPETU. Robert Hunter (d.1734), a Hunter of Hunterston, Ayrshire, was son of James Hunter, a son of the laird of that ilk. He was appointed lieutenant-governor of Virginia in 1707, but en route was captured by a French privateer and taken to France; he was, however, exchanged for the French bishop of Quebec soon afterwards. In 1710 he became governor of New York. Hunter was captain-general of Jamaica 1728–34. He married Elizabeth, daughter of Sir Thomas Orby, 1st Bart. of Croyland Abbey and widow of Brig.-Gen. Lord John Hay, and died in Jamaica.

His Excellency Robert Hunter Esqr Captain General & Chief Governour of Jamaica
A Johnston Sculp.

(Alexander Cumming, of Altyre), anonymous

Single coat Chippendale armorial, with Penrose in pretence. NIF, whereas F.7558, which reads "The Laird of Altyr's Arms", has no escutcheon of pretence. Alexander Cumming, of Altyre, Moray, married Grace Pearce, niece and sole heir of John Penrose of Penrose, Cornwall. Their son Alexander Penrose Cumming, of Altyre, assumed the additional surname of Gordon in accordance with the will of Sir William Gordon of Gordonstoun, Bart., whose heir he was. He succeeded to the Gordonstoun estate and was created a baronet in 1804.

Henry Home of Kames

Jacobean armorial (Home quartering Pepdie, Forrester and Ellem) F.15212. F.15213 is the same with "Judge in the Courts of Session & Justiciary" added. Henry Home (1696–1782), 3rd Laird of Kames, was the son of George Home 2nd of Kames and descended through the Homes of Renton from Sir David Home of Wedderburn, who was killed at Flodden. Lord Kames, a distinguished jurist, historian and author, was one of the major figures in Edinburgh's "age of enlightenment". Called to the Scottish bar in 1752, he became a Lord of Session the same year, and was Lord of Justiciary 1763–82. He had a house in the Canongate, and married Agatha, daughter of James Drummond of Blair Drummond, Perthshire, who in 1766 succeeded to that estate on the death of her nephew James. It was there that Lord Kames put into practice his revolutionary and highly successful agricultural theories. On his death Blair Drummond passed to his son George Home Drummond, who had assumed that additional surname, while the Kames estate was sold.

Sr William Baird of Newbaith Bart.

Jacobean armorial. NIF. A version (again NIF) has "Sr. William" erased from the copper. This was the second state, but Henderson Smith noted that there was also a third. Sir William Baird of Newbyth (or Newbaith), Haddington (1654–1737) was the only surviving son of John Baird of Newbyth (1620–98), Lord Lyon depute 1663, MP for Aberdeen 1665 and 1667, a Lord of Session as Lord Newbyth 1664–81 and 1689–98, who was thought to have received a baronetcy in 1660 on the restoration of King Charles II, though this is by no means certain. The family descended from the Bairds of Auchmedden, Aberdeenshire who had held those lands from 1534. William Baird was created a baronet of Nova Scotia in 1680, whilst his father was still alive. He married firstly Helen (d.1701), daughter of Sir John Gilmour, of Craigmillar, Lord President of the Court of Session, and secondly Mary, third daughter of Henry (St. Clair), Lord Sinclair. He died in Edinburgh, was buried at Liberton, and was succeeded by John (1685–1745), his first son and heir by his first wife. It must have been he who used the later states of the bookplate, for at his death without issue the baronetcy became extinct.

Sir Thos. Brand. Knt. Gentleman Usher of the Green Rod and Gentleman Usher Daily Waitr. to His Majesty Anno 1735

Jacobean quarterly armorial, with Campbell in pretence, within the chain of an officer of the Royal Household in Scotland, the crossed staffs of the Gentleman Usher in saltire behind. The 1st and 4th quarters of his arms pertained to his office; the 2nd and 3rd are Brand; and the escutcheon of pretence is for Campbell of Lundie. They were recorded at Lyon Office in 1721. F.3544. There are three variants. V.518 has only the first line of the inscription. V.519 is as the last but has the remainder of the inscription in ink, and so beautifully written that one might imagine it to be engraved. V.517 is similar to F.3544 but taken from the same copper as the illustration in the 1722 edition of Nisbet's *Heraldry*. Its use as an ex-libris is unascertained.

David Bethune of Balfour Esqr.

Jacobean armorial, its arms Bethune quartering Balfour of Balfour. NIF. David Bethune (d.1791), 16th Laird of Balfour, Fife, the son of Bethune of Bandon in the same county, married in 1709 his cousin Anne, daughter of David Bethune 13th Laird. On the death, in Rheims in 1717, of his brother-in-law James the 15th Laird, in exile following the 1715 Jacobite rising, David took possession of the family estate which should rightfully have passed to his cousin Rachel Campbell, Mrs. John Petullo, who he persuaded to resign her claim. David and Anne had two daughters, one of whom married David Bethune of Kilconquhar and so became ancestor to the Earls of Lindsay; the other married William Congalton of Congalton, Haddington, whose grandson eventually inherited Balfour and assumed the surname of Bethune.

The Armorial Bearing of the House of Abercairny (Moray)

Quarterly coat Jacobean armorial. NIF. There is also a smaller plate similarly signed, but somewhat later in date (NIF). The first known ancestor of the ancient baronial house of Moray of Abercairny was Sir William, one of the Barons of Scotland at the Convention of Birgham in 1289. His son Sir John acquired the lands of Abercairny as the tocher (dowry) of his second wife, Lady Mary, daughter of the 7th Earl of Strathearn. During the seventeenth century the family estates became encumbered partly due to its staunch Royalist loyalties, but William, the 12th Laird,

Henry Home of Kames

Sr. William Baird of Newbaith Bart.

Sir Thos. Brand Knt.
Gentleman Usher of the Green Rod
and Gentleman Usher Daily Waitr.
to His Majesty Anno 1735

David Bethune of Balfour Esqr.

The Armorial Bearing of the House of Abercairny.

William Urquhart of MELDRUM Esq.

managed to pay off all the mortgages and died in 1704. These bookplates belonged almost certainly to his son and successor James (1705–77), the 13th Laird, who managed to avoid any involvement in the Jacobite risings. He recorded these arms, Moray quartering Strathearn, *c.*1724 though they had probably been in use before that date. The crest of the sun rising above an earl's coronet possibly refers to the family claim to the earldom of Strathearn. For an account of this family's ex-libris see *The Bookplate Journal* for March 2006, pp. 19–29.

William Urquhart of MELDRUM Esqr.

Quarterly coat Jacobean armorial. F.30187. This is the second state, the first (F.30186) reading "William Urquhart, younger, of Meldrum Advocat. 1724". William Urquhart, 4th Laird of Meldrum, was the second but eldest surviving son of John, the 3rd Laird. He succeeded his father and

became chief of his name in 1741. In that year he recorded arms at Lyon Office without the quartering of Seton and with the addition of two greyhound supporters.

The Library of Innerpaffray Founded by DAVID Lord MADDERTY

Single coat Jacobean armorial. F.9087. The Franks Catalogue wrongly ascribes this plate to David Drummond (d. 1684), 3rd Lord Madderty, who founded Innerpeffery Library in 1660 at St Mary's Chapel, the family burial place near his home Innerpeffery Castle, near Crieff, Perthshire. By his will he endowed it with 5,000 merks (approximately £270) for its upkeep and that of the adjacent school. After his death a trust was set up to administer the endowment "for the education of the people, particularly young students in Strathearn" by William, 1st Viscount Strathallan, Lord Madderty's brother and heir. In 1751 the Right Reverend Robert Hay Drummond, bishop of St Asaph and later Bishop of Salisbury and Archbishop of York, erected a new building and left it his own important collection of books. It continued to operate as a lending library until 1968, by which time it had become obvious that the collection was too valuable to be used in that way. Since then it has operated as a reference library and museum, still managed by the trust. The ex-libris shows the arms as used by Lord Madderty, Drummond with a canton for Strathearn, ensigned with a baron's coronet, helm, crest and motto, and supported by two wild men holding clubs standing on a grassy compartment strewn with caltraps. On stylistic evidence the bookplate was engraved in the early decades of the eighteenth century.

John Earl of Hyndford 1743

Single coat Jacobean armorial. F.5153. He also used three other Jacobean plates (F.5150–52). John Carmichael (1701–67), 3rd Earl of Hyndford and 4th Lord Carmichael, succeeded his father in 1737, was a representative Peer for Scotland 1738–61, Sheriff Principal and Lord Lieutenant of Lanarkshire 1739, and Lord High Commissioner to the General Assembly of the Church of Scotland 1739–40. In 1741, on Silesia's invasion by the King of Prussia, he went as Envoy Extraordinary and Plenipotentiary to Prussia and was instrumental in arranging the Treaty of Breslau in 1742. The King of Prussia invested him with the Order of the Thistle on behalf of George II. He was also granted the right to add to his paternal arms the Eagle of Silesia and motto EX BENE MERITO, shown on the bookplate. In 1744 as envoy to Russia he assisted the Peace of Aix-la-Chapelle. Returning to Britain in 1750 he became a Privy Councillor and a Lord of the Bedchamber. Hyndford was an excellent landlord, spending considerable sums in improvements to his Lanarkshire estates. He married in 1732 Elizabeth (d. 1760), eldest daughter of Admiral Sir Cloudesley Shovell, widow of 1st Lord Romney; and secondly Jean, daughter of Benjamin Vigor.

His Grace James Duke of Atholl. Lord of Man & the Isles, Lord Strange &c. 1737

Jacobean armorial (quarterly coat with grand quarters) in the collar of the Order of the Thistle, with supporters, coronet, etc. F.21381 is a reprint. James Murray (1690–1764), third son of the 1st Duke by his first wife, Lady Catherine Douglas Hamilton, daughter of William, Duke of Hamilton and his wife, who was duchess in her own right. His elder brother having been killed at Malplaquet in 1709, and his father having procured an Act of Parliament vesting his honours and estates on James (his elder brother George having taken part in the 1715 and 1719 Jacobite risings and been attainted), he succeeded his father as 2nd Duke in 1724. However Lord George, when commanding the Jacobite forces in the 1745 rising and living at Blair Castle also assumed the Dukedom. In 1736 he succeeded his cousin, the 10th Earl of Derby, as 7th Baron Strange, and under that title he had a seat in the Lords. After Culloden he was taken prisoner, and he died in the Tower of London in 1746.

David Lyndesay of Glenesk Lethnot and Edzel

Quartered coat Jacobean armorial with supporters, etc. NIF. The Lindsays of Glenesk and Edzell stem from Sir David who succeeded to Edzell and the Barony of Glenesk, Angus, when Alexander, Master of Crawford, son of David, 8th Earl of Crawford was in 1530 excluded from the succession having pleaded guilty to "many crimes against his father". David was succeeded in 1542 by his cousin David, and he directed that after his death the Earldom and lands should be vested in Alexander's son David, whom he adopted. He became 10th Earl in 1558. The 9th Earl, however, had a family by his second wife, Catherine, daughter of Sir John Campbell of Calder, the elder of whom, Sir David, succeeded to Edzell and the barony of Glenesk. His direct male descendant was David Lindsay, who succeeded in 1671. See standard genealogical sources for further complications. Suffice it to say here that this bookplate almost certainly belonged to the David who was served heir in 1699, fell on evil days and sold the extensive barony of Glenesk to James 6th Earl of Panmure, and died impoverished in Kirkwall, Orkney in 1744. It seems odd, though, that a highly financially embarrassed gentleman, who is said to have become an ostler, would possess a library deserving such a grand ex-libris; but the earl's coronet upon the helm certainly alludes to the Earldom of Crawford to which the family had continued to lay claim.

The Armorial Bearings of the Right Honourable James Lord Somervell

Jacobean armorial F.27585, which also occurs printed in blue. Sgd: Tho. Calder fecit. Calder (fl. 1710–20), who also signed a bookplate for John Scott, was an Edinburgh engraver, who was working in the Abbey in 1732, in December of which year he was admitted to Sanctuary for debt at Holyroodhouse. James Somerville, or Somervell (1698–1765) was the eldest son of James Somerville of Drum, Midlothian, *de jure* 11th Lord, who like his three immediate predecessors did not claim or use the title. In 1721 he went to London and claimed the right to vote in the election of Scottish peers as heir to his great-great grand-father Hugh, 8th Lord, whose name had appeared on the roll in 1579. It was initially refused since no Lord Somerville had appeared on the roll of 1606. However, in 1723 his claim having been re-examined before the Committee of Privileges, it was allowed, and he duly voted as Lord Somerville. The next year he married a considerable heiress, Anne, only child of Henry Baynton of Spye Park, Wiltshire, and after her death, in 1734, another lady of fortune, Frances, daughter and coheir of John Rotherham of Much Waltham, Essex and widow of a successful East India merchant, Peter Curgenven. Somerville, an improving land-lord who greatly developed his estate at Drum, built a new house there to designs by Robert Adam, which is largely unaltered today. In 1730 the poet William Somerville, senior representative of the English Somervilles, who was financially embarrassed, resigned to James the family estates of Edstone, Warwickshire and Aston Somerville, Gloucestershire. James sold the former but made the latter his English home.

Robert Keith of Craig Esqr.

Jacobean armorial (F.16872). The Keiths of Craig descended from John, fourth son of William, 2nd Earl Marischal (d. 1483) and Mariota, daughter of Thomas, 2nd Lord Erskine. The arms were recorded at Lyon office in 1692 for Major Robert Keith of Craig, but with different crest and motto. It is said that the last male heir of this family died at Hammersmith in 1795.

His Grace
James Duke of Atholl,
Lord of Man & the Isles,
Lord Strange, &c. 1737.

Dabid Lyndesay of Glenesk
Lethnot and Edzel

The Armorial Bearing
of the Right Honourable
James Lord Somervell

Tho. Calder scu.

Robert Keith of Craig Esq.

ET MARTE ARTE

John Drummond

John Drummond

Jacobean armorial. NIF. Arms of Drummond of Pitkellony, otherwise Pitkellanie, Perthshire, a branch of Drummond of Concraig. Two examples of this bookplate, which dates from about 1720, have been researched. One is without inscription or with inscription cut off, leaving traces of the D for Drummond. The other, re-inscribed John Drummond, probably at a later date for an unidentified family member, is illustrated. It is possible that it was originally engraved for David Drummond, 11th Laird (1709–62), who succeeded his elder brother James (1701–23), who had died in a shipwreck. David married Mary, eldest daughter of Robert, 4th Lord Rollo, being succeeded by his second son, Robert, born 1733, captain in the 44th Regiment of Foot, serving in America. Robert sold Pitkellony and died in 1788 without legitimate issue.

Mr. Baron Maule

Jacobean mantled armorial (Maule quartering de Valonis, Barclay and Brechin, all within a bordure azure). The crest, a dragon vert spouting out fire before and behind, is usually shown with two legs only, which would really make it a wyvern. F.20044. John Maule (1706–81) of Inverkeillor, Forfar, became an advocate at the Scottish bar 1725, Keeper of the Register of Sasines 1737, MP for Aberdeen Burghs 1736–48, and was one of the Barons of the Exchequer in Scotland from 1748. Maule was the fifth son of Harry Maule of Kellie (d. 1734), a Jacobite who took part in the

rising of 1715, during which he rescued his elder brother James, 4th Earl of Panmure, who had been wounded and taken prisoner at the Battle of Sheriffmuir, and his grandfather was George, 2nd Earl of Panmure (d. 1671). John died unmarried.

The Arms of Her Grace Henrietta Dutches of Gordon

Lozenge armonal (Gordon impaling Mordaunt). F.12217. Lady Henrietta Mordaunt was the daughter of Charles. 3rd Earl of Peterborough who married in 1706 Alexander, 2nd Duke of Gordon (d. 1728). An intelligent and energetic lady, she undertook the management of the Scottish estates, as well as the upbringing of her large family. Among other agricultural improvements she introduced ploughs and ploughmen to work them. The Gordons had been Roman Catholics but the Duchess declared that she would like to bring up her children in the Protestant faith, and, as a result, in 1735 the Government settled on her a pension of £1,000 a year. This was, however, withdrawn in 1745 after she served breakfast for Prince Charles Edward when he passed the gates of Prestonhall, her house near Edinburgh, on his way to England.

Ann Countess of Aberdeen

Impaled armorial (Gordon of Haddo impaling Gordon quartering Badenoch, Seton and Fraser) on a mantle. NIF. Lady Ann Gordon (d. 1791), daughter of Alexander, 2nd Duke of Gordon, married in 1729, as his third wife, William Gordon, 2nd Earl of Aberdeen. She bore him four sons and a daughter.

(Elizabeth, Countess Home)

Anonymous Chippendale lozenge armorial (Home quartering Pepdie of Dunglass, with presumably Gibbons in pretence). F.15202. The daughter and heir of William Gibbons, of Vere, Jamaica, and widow of James Lawes, she married in 1742 William, 8th Earl Home (d. 1761). They had no children, and the Earl was succeeded by his younger brother Alexander. The inescutcheon is interesting as, though it is similar to the arms borne by some families of Gibbons, it also resembles the arms of Landells or Landale habitually borne on an inescutcheon by successive Earls Home in commemoration of the marriage of the 1st Earl (d. c.1490) with Mariota, daughter and heiress of Landells of that Ilk, Berwickshire. It is still so borne by the present Earl.

M.ʳ Baron Maule.

The Arms of Her Grace
Henrietta Dutches of Gordon

Ann Countess of Aberdeen.

Miss Mary Lillias Scott

Jacobean single coat armorial. F.26303. Mary Lillias Scott, daughter and coheir of John, 9th Laird of Harden, Roxburghshire, and his wife Jean Erskine, daughter of Alexander, 4th Earl of Kellie. They married in 1719. On his death without male issue in 1734, John was succeeded at Harden by his uncle Walter Scott of Whitefield. In Captain Keith Scott's *Scott 1118–1923* John of Harden is given three daughters: 1. Ann, who married Thomas Shairp of Houston; 2. Mary; 3. Lillias. In Balfour Paul's *The Scots Peerage* he is given two daughters unnamed. The bookplate suggests that the latter is correct. As John's coheiress and unmarried, Lillias could have been forgiven for making use of the undifferenced arms of Scott of Harden on a lozenge with helm, crest and supporters.

Anw. Lumisden

Allegorical pictorial-armorial. Sgd: R. Strange sculpt. F.18900. It has busts of Cicero and probably Sir Thomas Craig of Riccarton, countryman to both engraver and owner, who wrote on feudal laws and royal successions. The gesturing cupid below is amid books and judicial emblems, etc., and the Lumisden arms in a rococo cartouche on the left are as inconspicuous as the owner's name at base. Lumisden called it a "mark for my books". Sir Robert Strange (1721–92) was born at Pomona in Orkney of an ancient Flintshire family settled there. After fighting at Culloden he hid in the highlands, and then became a pupil of Le Bas in Paris, *c*.1746. The bookplate was probably engraved soon after his arrival there, and three years later he cut another pictorial ex-libris for its Scottish College. His only other one, the largest, was for Dr Thomas Drummond of Logiealmond, and depicts Aurora in danger of setting fire to the curtains above her (F.9138). Its designer T. Wale is elusive, and was perhaps the more familiar Samuel Wale. On returning to England, Strange devoted most of his talents to historical engraving. Andrew Lumisden (1720–1801), son of William Lumisden and descended from the Lumsdens of Cushnie, became private secretary to Prince Charles Edward after his arrival in Edinburgh, skulked four months in highland fastness after Culloden, and returned to Edinburgh wearing a black wig and as groom to a lady riding pillion. After going then to Paris and Rome he spent his latter years in Edinburgh. Sir William Stirling Maxwell recalled: "Persons still alive remember him as a lively, laughing old gentleman, with polished manners and stiff curls, an esteemed diner-out, a teller of pleasant anecdotes, and a maker of elaborate bows in foreign fashion". The bookplate brings to mind, incidentally, a memorably dangerous moment. Strange pursued by Hanoverian soldiers, rushed up the stairs of the Lumisden house at Duddingston, and Andrew's sister Isabella, who sat spinning, hid him under the great hoops of her chintz dress until the military departed. If true, it suggests that Strange was modestly built. It is said they were already affianced, but at any rate he returned to Edinburgh in 1747 to wed her and so became Andrew's brother-in-law.

(Dr. John Boswell). Anonymous allegorical armorial with crest. NIF. It occurs in both black and red.
John Boswell MD. Physician in Edinr. C.R.M.E. Soc. Rococo mantled armorial. NIF. V.457.
BOSWELLUS BOERHAAVIO PRAECEPTORI SUO. Portrait plate. F.3136.

These three all belonged to the same man, John Boswell (*c*.1706/8–80), the second son of James Boswell of Auchinleck and his wife Lady Elizabeth Bruce, daughter of the Earl of Kincardine He studied medicine at Leyden and graduated 1736. Licensed by the Royal College of Surgeons 1737, he became a fellow in 1748, and was later Censor. Boswell married Annie, daughter of Robert Cramond of Auldbar, Forfarshire. His nephew James, the biographer of Dr Johnson, twice referred to him in his text. In the latter, when he found his hero putting books in order in clouds of dust he said that it put him in mind of his uncle referring to the incomparable Samuel as "A robust genius born to grapple with whole libraries". The bookplates have strange emblems and inconsistencies. The first includes a cornucopia, Father Time, and an eager figure below avid for plenty. There is a gatherer of samphire – "dreadful trade" in the words of Edgar in King Lear – and a ship at sail beyond. Boswell's arms are an heraldic jumble. In the above's first quarter Boswell with the galley in base probably refers to Sinclair; the second quarter is Bruce, the third Abernethy. The fourth is elusive. Those on the large armorial are equally inaccurate, but first and fourth are Boswell of Auchinleck; the canton is for Sinclair, Earl of Orkney; and the second and third are Bruce, Earl of Kincardine and Abernethy. The cross engrailed refers to Sinclair, and the escutcheon to Auchinleck of that Ilk. The portrait on his third bookplate (see pp. 17 and 28) is of Boerhaave, the great teacher who made Leyden the leading school of medicine; and a mass of symbols occupy the surrounding circlet. Sgd: Begbie sct Edinr. Patrick Begbie was 1773–4 at Blyths Close, Castle Hill, Edinburgh, but seems to have

REPARABIT CORNUA PHŒBE

Miss. Mary Lillias Scot.

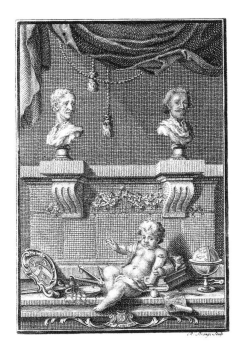

VRAYE FOY

PRO SALUTE

LABORE CÆLIQ. FAVORE

SI AUDES, ARDUA VINCES.

MANE VIGILA NOCTE QUE

IT IS ANE GUDE SPORT TO DOOE VEILE

John Boswell M.D. Physician in Edin.r C.R.M.E. &c.

settled in London c.1776, and for at least three years from 1777 he was at Dukes Court, St Martin's Lane. Most of his ex-libris work seems to have been in London, but he was probably sometime in partnership in Edinburgh, an armorial for Sir Charles Ross of Balnagowen (NIF) reading Begbie & Lee, Edin.

WM. BALDERSTON

Single coat Chippendale armorial. F.1274. Arms of Balderston of that Ilk. In *Alexander Nisbet's Heraldic Plates.* 1892, is one for George Balderston Appothecary & Chyrurgeon in Edinburgh, with the same arms but different crest and motto – appropriate to his calling. From the genealogy it seems likely that William, born 1688 could have been the elder son of George (died 1720). The arms are not recorded at Lyon Office.

Robert Oliphant Esgr. OF ROSSIE

Chippendale festoon (Oliphant impaling Buchanan). F.22288. Robert Oliphant (1718–95), of Rossie-Ochil, Perthshire, was Postmaster General for Scotland, and recorded arms at Lyon Office in 1777. He married Marian, daughter of Neil Buchanan of Hillington, Renfrewshire, MP for Glasgow Burghs, a nephew of Andrew Buchanan 1st of Drumpellier. The engraver hatched the Buchanan arms wrongly. They should have been Or a lion rampant

sable within a tressure flory counterflory gules, whereas those displayed on the impalement are the Royal Arms of Scotland.

Duke of Buccleugh (Scott)

Quarterly coat Chippendale armorial. F.26257, but there is another state NIF. The arms are interesting as the first grand quarter displays the undifferenced arms adopted by King James I and used by Charles I and Charles II, which would only have been appropriate were the Duke of Monmouth a legitimate son of Charles II. Subsequent Dukes have borne this quartering debruised with a baton sinister argent. This plate could have belonged to either the 2nd or 3rd Duke. Francis Scott, the 2nd Duke (1694–1751) was the only child of James, Earl of Dalkeith and of Lady Henrietta Hyde, his wife, daughter of Lawrence, Earl of Rochester, and grandson of James, Duke of Monmouth, son of Charles II by Lucy Walters, and of Anne, second daughter and heiress of Francis Scott, 2nd Earl of Buccleuch (d.1651), who succeeded her elder sister in the Earldom of Buccleuch and was created Duchess of the same. She was succeeded at her death by her grandson, Lord Dalkeith. In 1743 he obtained restoration of his father's forfeited Earldom of Doncaster and Barony of Scott of Tindale, though not the Dukedom of Monmouth. He was succeeded in all his honours by his grandson Henry (1746–1812), who also inherited the Dukedom of Queensberry in 1810, his grandmother having been Lady Jean Douglas, daughter of the 2nd Duke.

David Hume Esqr.

Single coat Chippendale armorial. F.15701. A very similar plate for him, from a different copper, is F.15702. David Hume (1711–76), the historian, philosopher, and leading figure in the "Scottish enlightenment", was second son of Joseph Hume, or Home, of Ninewells, Berwickshire. The name was spelt either way, but David insisted on the "U" as the more logical spelling considering the pronunciation. After travelling abroad in various capacities, often as secretary to diplomatic missions, with spells of writing at home, he became Librarian to the Faculty of Advocates in Edinburgh, succeeding Ruddiman (see p.62) in 1752. It allowed time and opportunity for research. His early philosophic works were not well received, which greatly disappointed him, but he turned increasingly to history, beginning with *Political Discourses* in that year, which proved popular, and went on to the first part of his ambitious *The House of Stuart*, which was less favoured as he dared to put Charles I in a good light. He resigned as Librarian in 1757. *The National History of Religion* did well, and in 1758 he produced *The House of Tudor*. In 1763 Hume joined the Earl of Hertford's Embassy in Paris as secretary until 1766, when he returned to England bringing Jean Jacques Rousseau with him. After being Secretary of State 1767–9 he felt he had enough money to retire to Edinburgh. The Humes of Ninewells arms were recorded at Lyon Office 1672–92, but are shown incorrectly on the bookplates, for the charges on the bordure should be fountains not hurts.

Thomas Carnegy Esqur. of Craigo

Single coat Chippendale armorial incorporating busy cherubs and a less than busy and stupid-looking ewe. F.5181. It was of English engraving, and of a familiar stock pattern. See the article on it by Carnegy Johnson in the *Ex-Libris Journal*, Vol.10, 1900, pp.8–11. Thomas Carnegy (1729–93) – the name is more usually spelt Carnegie – was the seventh but eldest surviving son of David Carnegie 3rd of Craigo (d.1761) and descended from Sir Robert Carnegie, 5th of Kinnaird, Senator of the College of

Justice as Lord Kinnaird, who was Ambassador to the Court of Henry II of France in 1550. These arms were matriculated at Lyon Office 1672–77 by Thomas's great-grandfather David, Dean of Brechin, who purchased Craigo. The bookplate was afterwards reprinted for a later Thomas of the family.

Cockburn of ROW-CHESTER

Chippendale, its arms Cockburn quartering de Vipont. F.6229. Thomas Cockburn (1723–87) of Rowchester, Berwickshire was a writer to the signet and deputy keeper of the Great Seal of Scotland. He acquired the lands of Rowchester, Bankhead and Scarlaw, all in the same county, and in 1779 recorded arms at Lyon Office. The eldest son of David Cockburn who, landless, was allowed to live at Langton, the seat of his kinsman Sir James Cockburn, 7th Bart., David was great-grandson of James Cockburn of Selburnrigg who fled abroad as a result of his involvement in the political events of 1688. The family descended from James Cockburn, first Laird of Selburnrigg, fifth son of Sir James of Langton (d. 1578). The crown and pen in the first quarter of the arms allude to Thomas's profession and office.

THO: RUDDIMAN A.M.Fac. Jurid.Edinb. BI-BLIOTHECARUS

A very individual design with triangles, one inverted, and monogram at centre. F.25655, but another version was from a different copper. Thomas Ruddiman (1674–1757), son of a farmer at Boyndie, Banffshire, was educated at the parish school and King's College, Aberdeen (MA 1694). In 1695 he became schoolmaster at Laurencekirk, but a chance meeting in 1699 with Dr Archibald Pitcairn, stranded there by bad weather, persuaded him to go to Edinburgh, where Pitcairn obtained for him a position in the Advocates' Library. He married Barbara Scollay in 1701, became assistant librarian the next year, then set up as a book auctioneer – as such selling the library of Pitcairn to Peter the Great of Russia. In 1714 he published *Rudiments of the Latin Tongue*, but his 1715 two-volume edition of the works of George Buchanan, with an assessment of his life and character, proved controversial. He went into a printing partnership with his brother Walter, and in 1729 acquired the *Caledonian Mercury* which remained in the family until 1772.

Wm. Douglas Esqr. Kinmaunt

Quarterly coat Chippendale. NIF. These arms were recorded at Lyon Office in 1668 for Sir William Douglas of Kelhead, Dumfriess-shire, second son of the 1st Earl of Queensberry who died 1673. His eldest son, Sir William (c.1675–1733) was created baronet 1705. This was presumably the ex-libris of his grandson, Sir William Douglas of Kelhead, 4th Bart. (c.1730–83), MP for Dumfriess Burghs 1768–80, who married in 1772 Grace, eldest daughter and co-heir of William Johnstone of Lockerbie. Their eldest son, Sir Charles, 5th Bart., succeeded his cousin the 5th Marquess of Queensberry in that title, and the second son, John, succeeded his brother on his death without male children in 1837, as 7th Marquess. Although this branch bore the territorial designation "of Kelhead" they seem to have lived at Kinmount (Kinmaunt) which afterwards became a seat of the Marquesses of Queensberry. Henry Alexander Douglas (1781–1837), younger brother of the 7th Marquess used the same, with the design reversed, as his bookplate, signed by Kirkwood.

Lord Prestongrange (Grant)

Chippendale armorial: Grant with Meldrum in pretence. F.12493. William Grant (c.1701–64) of Prestongrange, Haddington, was the second son of Sir Francis Grant of Cullen and Monymusk, Aberdeenshire, 1st Bart., a Senator of the College of Justice as Lord Cullen, and of Jean, his first wife, daughter of the Rev. William Meldrum of Meldrum. William Grant was, likewise, a Senator of the College of Justice, and was appointed Solicitor General for Scotland in 1737 and Lord Advocate in 1746. The following year he became MP for Elgin. In 1759 he matriculated arms at Lyon Office: Gules three antique crowns or on a canton argent a demi-otter issuant from a bar wavy sable all within a bordure ermine. Probably the engraver made a mistake, substituting the canton for an escutcheon.

John Straton Esqr.

Chippendale armorial. F.28367. The arms were recorded at Lyon Office in 1698 for Captain Charles Straton, the escutcheon in this instance not representing a marriage but being an integral part of the arms: Vairy on an escutcheon gules a fess in form of a wall crenellé of three pieces argent masoned sable.

ELIZABETH DUNDAS

Crest and motto. F.9304. Elizabeth Dundas (1795–1840) was the second daughter and third child of Sir Robert Dundas (1761–1842), Principal Clerk to the Court of Session and Deputy to the Lord Privy Seal in Scotland, by his wife Mathilda, daughter of Archibald Cockburn, a Baron of the Court of Exchequer in Scotland. She married in 1839 General Sir James Simpson. There is also a second similar bookplate as well as a circular one with just the crest.

Willm. Tytler writer to the Signet

Single coat Chippendale armorial. F.30132. William Tytler, writer in Edinburgh, married Jane, daughter of William Leslie and granddaughter of Sir Patrick Leslie of Iden. The Tytlers claimed descent from a member of the Seton family who, having killed a gentleman named Gray, fled to France and assumed the surname of Tytler. He and his two sons returned to Scotland with Queen Mary in 1560. The crest of Tytler, the sun hidden behind clouds, must refer to this legend as to the origin of the family, together with the motto "Occultus non extinctus" (Obscured but not extinct); but this was evidently a much later conceit, as such often were.

Whytt of Bennochy

Single coat Chippendale armorial. F.31675. In a later state (F.31669) the surname is changed to "Whyte", with a dexter hand holding a heart as crest, and the apt motto "Candidiora pectora". No doubt it was used by Whyte out of personal preference, since it was never recorded at Lyon Office. Of Scottish workmanship, it may well have been by the engraver of Lord Prestongrange's plate, above. Robert Whytt or Whyte of Bennochy, Fife (1714–66) became First Physician to the King in Scotland 1761, and President of the Royal College of Physicians, Edinburgh. Having studied at St Andrews, Edinburgh, London, Paris and Leyden, he became MD of the University of Rheims, and in 1736 was awarded the same at St Andrews. Made licentiate of medicine at the Royal College of Physicians, Edinburgh 1737, and a fellow of it the next year, he became Professor of Medicine at Edinburgh University in 1747, FRS in 1761, and the position of Physician to the King in Scotland was created for him. He was the author of numerous medical works. The family descended from Mathew Whyte of Maw, who had a charter of 1492 of the lands of Kilmaron, Fife. Robert Whyte, a merchant in Kirkaldy, and first Provost of the Burgh, acquired Bennochy. The arms were granted at Lyon Office in 1676. Dr Whyte's younger son John (1755–1813), who followed his brother at Bennochy, also succeeded to Strathkinness, Fife, and assumed the additional surname of Melville.

Sir Wm. Augustus Cunynghame of LIVINGSTONE, Bart.

Single coat Chippendale armorial. F.7611. Sir William Augustus Cunynghame (d.1828) of Milncraig, Ayrshire and Livingstone, Linlithgow, 4th Bart., was the only son of Sir David, of the same, 3rd Bart., and his wife Lady Mary Montgomerie, daughter of Alexander, 9th Earl of Eglington. He succeeded his father in 1767, was MP for Linlithgow 1774–90, and recorded arms at Lyon Office in 1775. Cunynghame became Clerk Comptroller of the Household in 1779, Comptroller of the Board of Green Cloth in 1797, and Receiver General of Crown Rents in 1806. He also used, incidentally, a Chippendale armorial (F.7610) and a crest plate (NIF), which occur printed in red.

John Straton Esq.r

Will.m Tytler writer to the Signet

Whytt of Bennochy

Sir W.m Augustus Cunynghame
of LIVINGSTONE Bar.t

Pref.s B Shelf 5' N.o 5'.

65

Archd. Swinton Esqr.

Single coat Chippendale armorial. F.28666. Captain Archibald Swinton (c.1730–1804), fourth son of John Swinton, 26th Laird of Swinton, Berwickshire, began as a surgeon's mate in an East Indiaman, arriving in India in 1752. He then transferred to the army's medical department for seven years, obtaining the rank of surgeon and his MD from St Andrew's University. In 1759 he joined the East India Company as an ensign, rising to captain in 1763. After serving with distinction in the Indian Wars he retired in 1766 due to wounds and bought the estate of Manderston in Berwickshire from the Humes in 1769 and in 1771 the Kimmerghame estate. He sold the former to Dalhousie

Watherstone in 1783, and the latter to Sir James Stirling, Bart. An ardent bibliophile, he built up a considerable library. His son, Archibald Campbell Swinton, used the same copper for his bookplate, changing the inscription and the arms to Swinton quartering Campbell.

John Adam. Architect

Single coat Chippendale armorial. F.115. His brother James's very similar plate is F.114. The family came of a line of minor Fife lairds since the fourteenth century. One, John Adam, fought at Flodden; another, Archibald, flourished in the reign of Charles I and exchanged the old estate of Fanno for Queen's Manor, also in Fife. His grandson, due to being "a bad economist" was forced to sell his land and, dying unmarried, was succeeded by his cousin John, builder in Kirkaldy, who had married Helen Cranstoun, a lady of good family. Their only son, William (1689–1748) became the most fashionable architect in Scotland, and he bought the estate of Blair in Angus and built a village which he named Maryburgh after his wife Mary, sister of William Robertson of Gladney. They were the parents of John (1721–92), Robert (1728–92), James (1732–94), all of whom became such eminent architects that their careers need no detailing here, and William, also an architect, but far less eminent. John and Robert jointly designed many superb

buildings in England and Scotland, whilst John, who inherited Blair Adam, as it is now called, lived there, once having to mortgage it to save his brothers from bankruptcy. The bookplate shows the arms recorded at Lyon Office in 1756 retrospectively in his late father's name. In 1765 John matriculated quite different arms, for Adam, quartering Robertson of Gladney. John used these, with Littlejohn in pretence, in his later bookplate (F.113), and James's plate is F.117. Both are now esquires rather than mere architects.

(Kerr, Marquess of Lothian)

Anonymous quartered coat armorial within the ribbon of the Order of the Thistle, with supporters, etc. NIF. Probably William Henry Kerr, 4th Marquess of Lothian (1710–75), KT 1768. Captain in the 1st Foot Guards 1741, ADC to the Duke of Cumberland 1745–46, he was wounded at the battle of Fontenoy 1745, commanded the Government Cavalry at Culloden 1746, and rose to be General in 1770. It could possibly, though, have belonged to his father, William, 3rd Marquess (c.1690–1767), who was a representative Peer for Scotland 1731–56 and Lord Clerk Register 1739–56. KT 1733/34. His first wife, William Henry's mother, was his cousin Jean Janet, eldest daughter of Lord Charles Kerr of Cramond, second son of the 1st Marquess.

Samuel Paterson Lukenbooths EDINBURGH

Small single coat Chippendale armorial within a linear rectangular frame. F.22888, but it occurs in two states. This bookplate owner is unidentifiable but uses the undifferenced arms of Paterson of Bannockburn, confirmed at Lyon Office 1672–98, and may or may not be related to that family. Lukenbooths were shops built near Edinburgh's old Tolbooth, demolished 1789, many of them against the

north elevation of St Giles. During the eighteenth century it was a prestigious area and became the centre of the printing and publishing trades. Here the poet Allan Ramsay opened his lending library, the first in Scotland, and he was followed by William Creech, publisher of the *Lounger* and the *Mirror*, to which most of Scotland's foremost writers contributed. The area degenerated early in the following century. The bookplate's crest might indicate an author, bookseller, or Writer to the Signet.

John Campbell Esqr. Cashier. Edinr.

Quarterly coat Chippendale armorial-pictorial, unicorns as quasi supporters, cheque, key, purse and cornucopia, etc. Dated 17–, but engraved by Richard Cooper, senior (see p. 28) in 1770. F.5016. John Campbell (d. 1777), known as "John of the Bank", joined the Royal Bank of Scotland on its foundation in 1727, became assistant secretary 1732, and was second cashier from 1734 until his death. Campbell was deputy Keeper of the Great Seal of Scotland. He was son of Colin Campbell of Ardmaddy, third son of the 1st Earl of Breadalbane and his second wife, Mary, daughter of Archibald, Marquess of Argyll. Colin was said never to have married, and his children therefore illegitimate, but apparently evidence exists to show that there was a marriage but that records were suppressed due to family disapproval. For a fuller account see *The Bookplate Journal*, September 1996, pp. 87–90.

ALEXR. INGLIS of Murdostoun

Quarterly coat Chippendale armorial (1 & 4 Inglis, 2 & 3 Hamilton of Inverdovat) with pictorial additions. F.16015. On matriculation at Lyon Office in 1734 Alexander was described as Hamilton alias Inglis of Murdiston, heir to his uncle Alexander Inglis of Murdostoun, Lanarkshire (d. 1719). He was also Laird of Inverdovat, later Tayfield, Fife, and son of Gavin Hamilton of Cleland and Isabel Hamilton, heiress of Inverdovat. Gavin recorded arms, Hamilton quartering Elphinstone. William Hamilton succeeded to Inverdovat on the death of his brother James in 1664, they being children of William Hamilton of Muirhouse and Anne, daughter of James Elphinstone of Inverdovat, descended from James Elphinstone, third son of Alexander 2nd Lord Elphinstone, who possessed Inverdovat by 1595. The naive creatures crouching aside the shield are not supporters but may have heraldic significance. The blasted oak stump sprouting shoots takes its theme from the crest and the motto INVICTUS MANEO,

ALEXᴿ. INGLIS of Murdostoun

ROBERT NISBET's

BIBLE.

COCKBURNSPATH,

JANUARY 14th 1768.

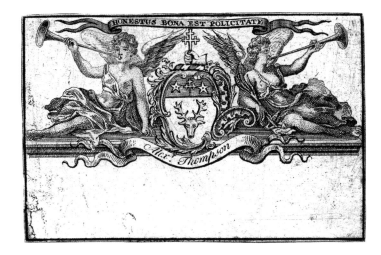

I remain unconquered, presumably by any disaster. One would love to know the significance of the empty goblet the dog clutches, but like much history the mists of time leave but tantalising references. Like John Campbell's bookplate above, this was surely of Cooper's engraving.

Alexr. Thompson

Single coat Chippendale armorial-pictorial, with trumpeting angels aside the arms, all resting on a bracket. NIF. The arms are those of Thomson, the usual spelling in Scotland, the Latin motto a version of the family's frequent one, "Honesty is a good policy". The crest is that of, amongst others, Thomson of Bonaly. What is unusual is the lower space within the border, which accords with other examples relating to merchants. A manuscript inscription below might have provided confirmation, but if he was, the motto was most apposite. The composition may also have served as a trade card.

ROBERT NISBETS BIBLE. COCKBURNSPATH, JANUARY 14th, 1768

Printed label within a rectangular border of ornaments. NIF. Ex Lee Collection. In view of its late date this is a surprisingly large printed label, and it occurs printed in both black and red. That leads one to suppose that he had the Old and New Testaments separately bound, but both prints were probably one-off and they indicate the respect which Nisbet had for the Holy Book. What strikes one also as unusual is that both he and Thomas Nicolson of Aberdeen, a century and a half earlier (see p. 8) were both of the same parish, for it was not a sizeable one. It was actually two

joined together – Cockburnspath and Old Cambus – and was on the lands of Dunglass but had no resident laird. Its ruined castle was on their property, and in 1834 it belonged to Sir John Hall of Dunglass, but it had previously been held by the Homes, who inherited it from the Pepdies.

Robt Ewing Baker GLASGOW

Oval engraved label ornamented by a festoon. NIF. Robert Ewing was admitted to the Incorporation of Bakers of Glasgow on 21 September 1769, at which time his address was 51 Trongate. He last appears in their records in 1799. Other familiar Scottish oval labels of the same period include Robt. Barbour GLASGOW, which incorporates an urn at the top, A. Hamilton, Alexr. McCallum GREENOCK, and WILLIAM NICOL TAYLOR, ABERDEEN, JULY 1797, but there are numerous others.

John Willison M.D. Dundee

Chippendale engraved label. NIF. The Willisons seem to have been essentially Inverness people, and it is possible that John was the one baptised there on 14 September 1728, the son of John Willison and Janet Morton who married 1 January 1725. Doctors, like clergymen, were in professions which must often have taken them far from home in pursuance of a career.

NB. These three labels give a glimpse of the diversity of Scottish examples during the course of only several decades. Some were printed, but during the rococo style's popularity engraved or etched alternatives came into their own, and festoon plates were soon to enjoy popularity.

Some, charmingly, declare pride in profession or business, and a naive example for a blacksmith is appended above. Love of books amongst literate people happily knew and knows no bounds.

Sigillum universitatis doctorum magistrorum et scolarium sancti andree

Pictorial, copied from the ancient seal of St Andrews University which must have been made not later than 1418, for the arms above the canopy with the crescent moon are those of Peter de Luna, who, as Anti-Pope Benedict XIII of Avignon (1394–1417) confirmed the foundation of the University by a papal bull dated 28 August 1413. A Regent Master at a desk on the dexter side is reading and expounding to a class of seven students seated at a table on the sinister side. In the intervening space, below St Andrew on the cross, is the Bedellus, seated, and holding a mace. Over the dexter canopy are the Royal Arms of Scotland, and over the sinister the arms of Bishop Wardlaw. F.33637. The same subject features on other ex-libris of the University, and on stamps for the boards of books. Wardlaw was the first Chancellor there. Before the Reformation there were numerous colleges, mostly dedicated to theology, though other subjects were taught. The library was founded in 1611 with lands transferred from the church. The University declined in importance in the eighteenth century as that of Edinburgh increased, but revival followed in the nineteenth.

VIA VERITAS VITA

AB ANIMO DISPELLERE CALIGINEM

Bibliotheca Universitatis Glasguensis

Bibliotheca Universitatis Glasguensis

Armorial in an oval with Minerva and probably Erato supporting. F.33565–7, three different plates of similar composition. The incorporated symbols have appeared from time immemorial on the arms of the city, which were to be officially granted by Lyon Burnett in 1866. They did not include the mace, the Royal Crown and the head of St Kentigern (or Mungo), the patron saint. The 1900 University arms show the mace, the book, the tree with a redbreast and the bell. Most is summed up in the old verse: "The fish that never swam, The tree that never grew, The bell that never rang, And the bird that never flew". They relate to incidents in the saint's life. As a boy at Culross he restored to life a pet robin which his companions had torn in pieces, and kindled a fire with a frozen oak branch. Later the Queen of Cadzow was suspected of unfaithfulness by her husband, King Redderech. He found a ring he'd given her in the culprit's possession, threw it into the river Clyde, then demanded his spouse return it. She appealed to Kentigern, promising penance, so he sent a monk down to fish and bring back the first he caught alive. Lo and behold, the ring was in its mouth, so he returned it to her, and all was well. See the following for comment on the University.

In Classe Discipulus INGENIO AC LABORE Insignis PRAEMIUM HOCCE … Apud Coll Glasg. Imo die. Maii

Pictorial premium or prize bookplate depicting frontage, entrance and tower. There are two differently engraved plates, of which this is the second. NIF. The first is signed "Swan Sculpt", i.e. Joseph Swan of Glasgow, 30 ex-libris by whom Fincham lists – though there were assuredly many more. This one shows a more robust entrance, level chimneys, and figures in the foreground, etc. It was in use, as you see, by 1859. See Lee, *Premium or prize ex-libris*. 2001, p.40, where both plates are illustrated. Glasgow College and Glasgow University were one and the same, called either indiscriminately. In 1451 James II of Scotland persuaded Pope Nicholas V to authorise Bishop Turnbull of Glasgow to set up a university there, to join the 40 year old St. Andrews University and thus give Scotland, like England, two universities. Modelled on the University of Bologna, at first it was housed in various buildings in the Blackfriars area, and Mary Queen of Scots granted it the manor of Blackfriars in 1563. In *c*.1656 the building depicted was erected along the High Street, and later a court was added behind for the professors' houses. In 1865 the

University moved to Gilmorehill, the old building was sold, and it was demolished *c.*1880. Swan worked at three different addresses in Trongate 1818–34 and then at various other addresses until his death in 1872. Born in Glasgow in 1796, he took over the business of Charles Dearie in 1818, was twice married, and published *Select Views of Glasgow and its environs*, Glasgow 1843.

SPOTTISWOODE. 17-

A most curious, but naively charming, plate showing a gigantic eagle on diminutive mountains apparently about to attack the sun. It is of course based on the crest of Spottiswoode of that Ilk: An eagle displayed gules looking towards the sun in splendour. The motto is correct for that family, but the arms displayed on the eagle's breast have an ermine ground, and also lack the chevron gules. However, the family arms were not recorded at Lyon Office until 1814, and one suspects that the chevron was introduced then. Dated 17–, with blanks for addition of the two last digits, the print illustrated, which belonged to F.J. Thairwall, is completed to read 1778. It was probably, however, engraved for John Spottiswood (1666–1728) who in 1700 repurchased the lands of Spottiswood which had been sold by his great-grandfather John, Archbishop of St Andrews, 1615–21, and Lord High Chancellor of Scotland, 1635–39. This John was a distinguished advocate at the Scottish Bar, and married in 1710 the Hon. Helen Arbuthnott, daughter of Robert, 2nd Viscount of Arbuthnott. Prior to the sale the family had been Lairds of Spottiswood from at least the thirteenth century. F.27749.

Hew Scott A.M.

A bookpile incorporating a bust of John Knox at top centre. Unusually, instead of an armorial at centre there is only crest and motto. F.26287. The print illustrated here, from the Pincott Collection, has "D.D." and "of West Anstruther" added in manuscript. See *Bookpile Bookplates*, 1992, where this and Scottish bookpiles for William Cullen, MD, and Thomas Rigg, Advocate, are illustrated and described. Hew Scott (1791–1872), son of Robert Scott, an excise officer, was born at Haddington and studied at Edinburgh and Aberdeen Universities, graduating MA from the latter. He collated old ecclesiastical records at the Register House in Edinburgh, was licensed to preach by Haddington Presbytery, and though ordained to a Canadian mission in 1829 was persuaded to remain in Scotland. He ministered at Garvald, Ladykirk, Cockpen and Temple, and was preferred in 1839 to the charge of West Anstruther, Fife, where he died. DD of St Andrews, his great work was *Fasti Ecclesiae Scoticanae*, 6 vols, 1866–71, an exhaustive and most scholarly production. In habit, though, he was distinctly eccentric and miserly.

Georgius Cock Societ:Reg:Phy. Edin.Soc.

Pictorial showing a classical female figure festooning an urn, a snake as symbol of eternity on its right. F.6222. Franks noted that it was in Ovenden's book, and T. Ovenden was an engraver in London 1790–1813; but the plate was the work of Hampson, Prince and Cattle of York and some prints bear their signature.

JAMES ARBUTHNOT Junr. Apothecary, Chemist & Druggust PETERHEAD

Pictorial with figures aside the central oval, with indication of perhaps boiling up medicines and gathering herbs. It may have served the purpose of a trade card as well as an ex-libris. NIF.

Sir William Forbes Bart. of Pitsligo

Quarterly spade shield armorial in an oval. F.10938. He earlier used a Chippendale single coat armorial dated 1760 (NIF). Sir William Forbes (1739–1806) of Pitsligo, Aberdeenshire which he inherited through his paternal grandmother, 6th Bart., succeeded his father Sir William in 1743. He was partner in the Banking House of Forbes, Hunter & Co., Edinburgh, and was prominent in the literary circles of that capital. He wrote the biography of his friend the poet James Beattie (1735–1803), acquired considerable land adjacent to the Pitsligo estate and became one of the foremost land improvers of his day. In 1771 he married a lady described as "the beautiful and truly admirable Miss Elizabeth Hay", daughter of Sir James Hay of Haystoun, 4th Bart.

Robert Drummond

Festoon armorial: quartered coat, Drummond and augmentation for Strathallan, with a mullet for cadency at centre point. F.9133. The Hon. Robert Drummond (1728–1804), of Cadland, Hampshire, was the third son of William, 4th Lord Strathallan, who was killed at the Battle of Culloden in 1746 fighting for Prince Charles Edward Stuart, the Young Pretender. As a young man, in 1744, with his brother Henry, he was sent to London to their uncle Andrew Drummond, in whose bank Robert became a partner in 1749. He married Winifred Thompson. Andrew Drummond, a goldsmith, began banking at the Golden Eagle on the east side of Charing Cross in 1717. Often called "the Jacobite Bank" his customers included many aristocratic Scots. His business flourished, he gave up his goldsmith's business in 1737, and in 1760 he moved to the west side of Charing Cross. After his death in 1769 the family remained sole proprietors, and their customers included George III and Josiah Wedgwood. Drummond's Bank was rebuilt in 1877–9, and acquired by the Royal Bank of Scotland in 1924.

(Trotter)

Anonymous spade shield armorial (Trotter quartering Trotter) of unusual elegance. NIF. Probably originally the bookplate of Thomas Trotter (1761–93), 7th of Mortonhall, who matriculated arms at Lyon Office in 1792, this ex-libris was certainly used also by later representatives of the family, and it has been regularly illustrated in successive editions of *Burke's Landed Gentry*. Thomas Trotter was the third son of John Trotter, 5th of Mortonhall (1667–1718), of a family established in Edinburgh as merchants in the sixteenth century and descended from the Trotters of Catchelraw, Berwickshire, considerable landowners in that county from the fourteenth century. Both quarterings have been used by this family, the first one recorded at Lyon Office in 1678, though the matriculation of 1792 seems the first time they were shown quartered.

Brisbane

Crest with festoon and motto. NIF. This is the crest of the ancient family of Brisbane of Brisbane, Ayrshire, so styled since the first half of the seventeenth century, but before that seated at Bishopton in Renfrewshire since at least the middle of the fourteenth. This was probably the ex-libris of Thomas Brisbane (c.1723–1812), who succeeded his uncle in the Brisbane estates in 1770. His wife was Eleanor, daughter of Sir Michael Bruce of Stenhouse, Bart. She was one of six sons and seven daughters, and her mother was Mary, daughter of General Sir Andrew Agnew, Bart., of Lochnaw. The Scots had an eye for good marriages as well as pride in longevity of kinship. That perhaps accounts for the modesty of this composition, for if you are assured of your standing and status you don't need puff; but not overspending may have been part of the economic equation. Thomas's famous son's bookplate follows later.

Sir Hugh Munro
of Fowlis Bar.ᵗ 1782.

Sir Hugh Munro, of Fowlis Bart. 1782

Spade shield armorial (Munro quartering Seymour) within the ribbon of a baronet of Nova Scotia from which the badge depends; with supporters, etc. F.21341. Sir Hugh Munro (1763–1848) of Foulis, Ross-shire, 8th Bart., was the elder son of Sir Harry Munro, 7th Bart., and of Anne, his wife, daughter of Hugh Rose of Kilravock, and grandson of Lt.-Col. Sir Robert Munro, 6th Bart., who was killed at the battle of Falkirk in 1745, and of Mary his wife, daughter and heir of Henry Seymour of Woodlands, Dorset.

(Hay. Marquess of Tweeddale)

Anonymous spade shield armorial (Hay impaling Maitland) with supporters, etc. on a mantle, coronet above. Sgd: Kirkwood & Son Sculp., for comment on whom see p.18. NIF. George Hay, 7th Marquess of Tweeddale (1753–1804), succeeded in 1787. He married in 1785 Lady Hannah Charlotte Maitland, daughter of the 7th Earl of Lauderdale. Lord Lieutenant co. Haddington and a Representative Peer 1796–1804, he and his wife died of fever in the fortress of Verdun, where they were imprisoned by Napoleon.

CHAS. SHARP OF HODDOM ESQR.

Single coat spade shield armorial in an oval bearing the inscription, with festoon and wreath. F.26568. Almost certainly the plate of Charles Kirkpatrick Sharpe, as usually spelt (1750–1813), of Hoddom, Dumfriess-shire, only son of William Kirkpatrick of Aibland (1705–78), who assumed the surname of Sharpe on inheriting the estate from his uncle Matthew Sharpe, and of Jean, his wife, daughter of Charles Erskine of Alva. By his marriage in 1770 to Eleanora, daughter of John Renton of Lamberton, Charles was the father of Lt.-Gen. Matthew Sharpe (d.1846), Charles Kirkpatrick Sharpe (c.1781–1851), the antiquary, artist and poet known as the Scottish Horace Walpole, Vice-Admiral Alexander Renton Sharpe (1785–1860) and William John Sharpe (1797–1860), a sporting celebrity of his day. All dying without issue, Hoddom was sold in 1878 to Edward Brook.

MacLeod Bannatyne ESQR.

Spade shield armorial (Bannatyne quartering MacLeod). Sgd: J. Archer Sculp. F.1378–9. The second state differs in the engraving of the castle. James Archer, engraver in Edinburgh, was at Parliament Close in 1790 and Anchor Close 1793–7. He married Janet, daughter of Archibald Lethem, in 1786. Sir William MacLeod Bannatyne (1743–1833) was the only son of Roderick MacLeod and Isabella, née Fairholm, whose mother Marion was daughter and heiress of Hector Bannatyne of that Ilk and Kames. Lord of Session as Lord Kames 1799–1823, in which year he was knighted, he was a notable figure in literary Edinburgh, contributing papers to *The Mirror* and *The Lounger*, was a founder of the Highland Society in 1784, and of the Bannatyne Club, to which he gave his name. On succeeding his uncle James at Kames in Bute in 1795 he assumed the surname Bannatyne in lieu of MacLeod and matriculated arms, but due to his extravagant life-style had to part with his estate. The Bannatynes descend from Gilbert McAmelyne in the thirteenth century, whose son and grandson were granted lands in Bute and Ayrshire. Sir William's MacLeod descent derived from the wife of his ancestor Ninian Bannatyne of Kames, Mary, daughter of Duncan Campbell younger of Auchinbreck and of Mary. daughter and heir of William MacLeod of MacLeod.

GEO. CHALMERS ESQ. F.R.S.S.A.

Spade shield armorial. F.5491. George Chalmers (1742–1823), historian, antiquary, political and biographical writer, descended from the Chalmers of Pittensear, Moray. He was educated at the grammar school at Fochabers, King's College, Aberdeen and Edinburgh University where he studied law. In 1763 he went to Maryland to join his uncle who had inherited land, settling in Baltimore as a lawyer. He returned in 1775 to London, where he remained. In 1786 he was appointed Chief Clerk of the Committee of Privy Council for Trade and foreign plantations, and he became FRS in 1791. His principal works were biographies of Daniel Defoe, Thomas Paine, Thomas Ruddiman (see p. 62) and Mary Queen of Scots. He also published editions of the poetry of Sir David Lyndsay and of Allan Ramsay, and the first three volumes of a proposed five volume history of Scotland titled *Caledonia*.

James Dickson Esqr. of Ednam in the County of ROXBURGH

Spade shield armorial. NIF. James Dickson (1712–71) was born at Stitchell, the youngest son of James Dickson, and his wife Jean, also a Dickson. In youth he is said to have broken the Pantwell in Kelso Square and fled to London where he became a naval agent and made a fortune. Returning to Kelso, he built Havannah, later Ednam, House and acquired the nearby Ednam estate from the Edmonston family in 1761. Three years later he bought Broughton, Peeblesshire. The arms are unrecorded at Lyon Office though similar to those of various Dickson families. The impalement is meant for Hogg, for his wife was Mary Hogg. He was succeeded by his nephew Captain William Dickson RN (later Admiral), son of his brother Archibald. Broughton was sold in 1774, and Ednam House was bought by the Douglasses of Springwood. It is now a popular fishing hotel.

James Edward Urquhart Esqr.

Spade shield trophy armorial. F.30184, James Edward Urquhart (1747–1811) was second son of John Urquhart 1st of Craigston, Aberdeenshire, and of Cromarty, and Jean, daughter of William Urquhart 21st of Meldrum. He matriculated the arms 1803. Ensign in the 14th Regiment of Foot, 1762, he rose to be Major-General in 1798. Urquhart was Town Major of the garrison at Boston, Mass. 1775–76, and became Commander of Fort Charles, Port Royal in Jamaica in 1783. He married at Boston in 1775 Hannah, daughter of Thomas Flucker of that city, but in 1786 divorced her for adultery with Capt. Stephen Kemp of the Marines. The next year he married Elizabeth Davies. His earlier spade shield bookplate (F.30183) shows the ancient arms of Urquhart of Cromarty impaling presumably Flucker. See Paul Latcham, *Bookplates in the Trophy Style*, 2005 for fuller details.

SCOTT OF HARDEN

Spade shield armorial with self-regarding mermaids as supporters. Sgd: D. Lizars Sculpsit. F.26260. Walter Scott (1724–93), 11th Laird of Harden, Roxburghshire, was the eldest son of Walter Scott, 10th Laird (1682–1746) by his third marriage, to Anne, daughter of Jon Scott of Gorranberry. The Scotts of Harden descended from William Scott, generally known as 1st Laird, though the Harden lands were acquired in 1501 by his father Robert

NEC CITO NEC TARDE

MURUS AHENEUS

Archer Sculp.

MacLeod Bannatyne ESQ.ᴿ

SPERO

GEO. CHALMERS ESQ.
F.R.S.S.A.

FORTIS JUVAT

FORTUNA

James Dickson Esqr.
of Ednam in the
County of ROXBURGH.

DUM SPIRO SPERO

James Edward Urquhart Esqr.

Scott of Stirches, who had confirmation of the lands and barony of Harden from Lord Home in 1535. Walter Scott of Harden married in 1754 Lady Diana Hume Campbell, third daughter of the 3rd Earl of Marchmont and 3rd Lord Polwarth, who on the death of her niece Ann in 1822 became *de jure* 5th Lady Polwarth, which peerage had been created in 1690, in remainder to "heirs male of the body and heirs of the said heirs", though she never claimed or used the title. Their only surviving son, Hugh Hepburne Scott, successfully claimed the Lordship of Polwarth in 1835 and became ancestor of the subsequent Lords Polwarth.

Jas. Robertson Esqr. of Lude

Spade shield armorial. Unsigned. NIF. James Robertson (d. 1803), 13th Laird of Lude, Perthshire, served heir to his father, John, in 1758. He married in the same year his cousin Margaret, eldest daughter of the Hon. Robert Mercer, formerly Nairne. The Robertsons of Lude, senior chieftains of the clan Robertson, descended from Patrick, who received the barony of Lude from his father Duncan of Atholl, 1st chief of clan Donnachaidh (Robertson), who died post 1355. The bookplate shows the arms of Robertson of Lude impaled with those of Mercer quartering Nairne and Murray, and the unique crest of the Lude family, a sleeping dog with the motto "dinna waken sleeping dogs".

Ja. Robertson Esq. of Lude.

George Paterson of Castle Huntly Esq.

George Paterson of Castle Huntly Esqr.

Spade shield wreath armorial (Paterson impaling Gray).
F.22879. George Paterson, MD (1734–1817) went to India
as official secretary to Sir John Lindsay and then to Sir
Richard Harland, and distinguished himself in the
transaction of difficult negotiations with the court of
Arcot. Returning in 1776 he recorded arms at Lyon Office,
and in the same year married the Hon. Anne Gray, sixth
daughter of 11th Lord Gray. In 1777 he bought the Castle
of Lyon in the Carse of Gowrie, which he called by its
original name Castle Huntly. It had been built by his wife's
ancestor 1st Lord Gray in 1452, and had subsequently
belonged to the Earls of Strathmore.

Halkerston of that Ilk

Spade shield armorial. F.13279. The family of Halkerston,
often spelt Hackston, styled of that Ilk, were seated at
Rathillet in Kilmany parish, Fife from 1635 until towards
the end of the eighteenth century when Hellenus
Halkerston recorded arms at Lyon office in 1772, and it
seems probable that he was owner of the bookplate.

THE HONBLE. William Craig one of the Lords of Council and Session and Lord Commissioner of Justiciary

Single coat spade shield armorial, with helm, crest and
motto. F.7215. The arms are those of Craig of Riccarton,
Midlothian, with a bordure gules for difference, not
recorded at Lyon Office. William Craig (1746–1813) was the
eldest son of the Rev. Dr. William Craig, a minister at
Glasgow. He studied at Edinburgh University and became
an advocate at the Scottish bar in 1768. In 1784 he was
appointed Advocate-Depute and held that office until 1787,
when he was made Sheriff-Depute of Ayrshire. On the
death of Hailes in 1792 he was raised to the bench as Lord
Craig, and he was three years later made a judge of the
court of judiciary, holding office until 1812. Progress of
his career was slower than it might have been, because
of his literary preoccupations and activities. He belonged to
a literary society called the Tabernacle. It met for reading
and discussion in a tavern, then changed its name to the
Mirror Club and published the *Mirror* on Tuesdays and
Saturdays – but it was short-lived. He was also a regular
contributor to the *Lounger*, later published by the same.

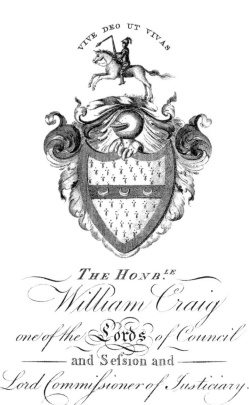

ROBERT MOUBRAY ESQr: of Cockairny

Single coat spade shield festoon armorial. NIF. There were three successive Lairds of Cockairney, Fife, called Robert whose bookplate this might have been: Robert (1770–79), 4th Laird; his son Robert (d. 1794), 5th Laird, and Lt.-Col. Sir Robert (1774–1848), Knight of Hanover, DL and JP for Fife. The most likely is the second Robert, who was the eldest surviving son of his father and his wife (and cousin) Mary, only child and heir of James Dudgeon of Inverkeithing. His grandfather was John Moubray of the same (d. 1732), 3rd Laird, whose wife Margaret was daughter of the Rev. John Minnaird, minister of East Calder.

Maxwell of Pollok & Calderwood

Spade shield armorial with two supporters, crests and mottoes. F.20239. This strange heraldic chimera must be the bookplate of Sir William Maxwell of Calderwood, 6th Bart., born in 1748, who died without issue in 1829. It combines armorials of two Maxwell families, of Pollok, Renfrewshire and Calderwood, Lanarkshire, the shield being impaled. One supporter is a Pollok monkey, the other a Calderwood stag; one crest is the stag's head of Pollok, the other the man's head of Calderwood. Both mottoes are used, and dependent from the arms is the ribbon and badge of a baronet of Nova Scotia, a distinction shared by both

families. The purpose of this bizarre marshalling must have been to emphasise the fact that Sir William was the lineal heir male of the Maxwells of Pollok, of which estate he felt he should have been proprietor, but was not. As it was, his distant kinsman Sir John Maxwell of Pollok, 7th Bart. (1768–1844), who had succeeded in 1785, was proprietor. The common ancestor of both baronets was Sir John Maxwell of Nether Pollok, Dryps and Calderwood (late 14th century).

John Leith Ross of ARNAGE & BOURTIE

Many-quartered spade shield armorial of Ross, with Anderson in pretence. F.25540. John Leith Ross (1777–1839) of Arnage, Aberdeenshire and of Bourtie in the same county, was DL and a writer to the signet. Lt.-Col. of the Ellon Volunteers, in 1803 he succeeded his aunt Christian Ross of Arnage in that estate. He was the only son of Alexander Leith of Freefield and Glenkindie and of his second wife Martha (d. 1777), daughter and coheir of John Ross of Arnage (1707–89), who was deaf and dumb. The Rosses of Arnage descended from the Rosses of Auchlossie, Aberdeenshire, seated there from early in the fifteenth century.

CUMMING GORDON OF ALTYR & GORDONSTOWN BART.

Spade shield armorial (Cumming quartering Penrose with an escutcheon of Gordon quartering Sutherland, as recorded at Lyon Office in 1795). Grant of an escutcheon showing a full achievement is most probably unique, so it is pleasing to find it appearing on this family's bookplates. Sgd: Kirkwood. F.12254. Sir Alexander Penrose Cumming, 1st Bart. (d.1806), eldest son of Alexander Cumming, of Altyre, Moray, and his wife Grace Pearce, niece and sole heir of John Penrose, of Penrose, Cornwall, married in 1773 Helen, the daughter of Sir Ludovick Grant, Bart. of Grant. Early in life he joined the 13th Regiment, and he was later Lt.-Col. of the Strathspey Fencibles, receiving the thanks of the C.-in-C. for suppressing an affray at Dumfries in 1794. Cumming succeeded to the estates of Sir William Gordon of Gordonstown, last Bart., in 1795 and assumed the name and additional arms of Gordon. He was created a Baronet in 1804.

SIR JAMES STEWART DENHOLM Baronet of Coltness & Westshiel

Quarterly coat armorial (Stewart quartering Denholm) within an oval framed by the motto and badge of a baronet of Nova Scotia, with supporters, etc. F.8447. Sir James Steuart Denham, or Stewart Denholm (1744–1839), of Coltness, Lanarkshire, 8th Bart. and 3rd Bart. of Goodtrees, was the only son of Sir James Steuart of

Coltness, who had succeeded his father in the Goodtrees baronetcy in 1727 and his cousin Sir Archibald Steuart Denham in the Coltness one in 1773. This Sir Archibald had inherited the Coltness baronetcy from his nephew in 1759 and also became, by special remainder, 2nd baronet on the death of his maternal uncle Sir William Denham, 1st Bart. In 1773, although the Steuart baronetcy of Coltness passed to Sir James as has been mentioned, the Denham one went to a maternal relative. However, in 1776 Sir James inherited the Denham estates and assumed the additional surname of Denham. He had sold the estate of Goodtrees in 1756. He recorded these arms at Lyon Office in 1810.

Sir William Maxwell of Monreith Bart.

Single coat spade shield armorial within the ribbon and badge of a baronet of Nova Scotia, framed by a wreath. F.20101. The escutcheon is part of the family arms, not one of pretence. Sir William Maxwell, 4th Bart. (d. 1812) was the only son of Sir William Maxwell of Monreith, 3rd Bart (*c.*1715–71), and of Magdalen, his wife, daughter of William Blair of Blair, Ayrshire (formerly Scott). He married in 1776 his cousin Katharine (d. 1798), daughter and heiress of David Blair, of Adamton, Ayrshire. She bore him two sons and three daughters. Monreith is in Wigtownshire.

Sir Alexr. Jardine of Applegarth Bart.

Pictorial-spade shield armorial, the supporting horse and gentleman, who is apparently in shining armour, within a romantic landscape; the shield rests against a rock on which is set the crest, the motto scroll on the ground in front. Though they are the granted supporters, a horse at liberty and a man in armour (who should properly have a scimitar at his side), it is fun to see them depicted in less than formal mode. F.16313. Sir Alexander Jardine (d. 1821), 6th Bart. of Applegarth, Dumfriesshire, only son and heir of Sir William and his wife Barbara de la Motte, a French lady, succeeded his father in 1807. He married in or before 1799 Janet, daughter of Thomas Maule, Lieutenant of Invalids, grandson of Henry Maule, Bishop of Meath. His eldest son succeeded him. It is odd that the bookplate's arms lack indication of the baronetcy.

GUTHRIE of GUTHRIE

Spade shield quarterly coat armorial. NIF. (The Chippendale armorial similarly inscribed and also with supporters is F.13114). The Guthries derive their name from Guthrie, near Forfar in Angus. In 1457 Alexander Guthrie acquired Kincaldrum in Angus from the 1st Earl of Rothes. His son, Sir David, obtained a Royal Charter of the barony of Guthrie from James III in 1465, and from then the family have been generally known as "of Guthrie" or "of that Ilk". The owner of the bookplate was probably John Guthrie, the 16th Laird, who recorded arms at Lyon Office in 1772 (not 1799 as in *Burke's Landed Gentry*) though they had already been long in use. They are quarterly 1 & 4, Or a lion rampant gules armed and langued azure, 2 & 3, Azure a garb or, said to be derived from Cumin. The supporters were also granted then. Sometimes the arms are given (as in Nisbet) 1 & 4, Argent a cross sable, 2 & 3, Azure three garbs or. John married Margaret, daughter of the Rev. Mr. Whyte of Murroes.

Stephen Freeman, Esq. Physician, e Collegio Regio Aberdonensi. was honoured with the degree of Doctor in Physic at the above University, the 23d. of Augt. MDCCLXXX

Single coat spade shield armorial on a mantle. NIF. It was necessary then for those who applied for doctorates to have recommendations from respected people, and in the case of Freeman they were Drs. William Vaughan and Henry Brown. See P.J. Anderson, *Officers and Graduates of the*

Sir Alexᵣ Jardine, of Applegarth Barᵗ

STO PRO VERITATE

GUTHRIE of GUTHRIE

Stephen Freeman, Esqᵣ
Physician,
è Collegio Regio Aberdonensi,
was honoured with the degree of Doctor in
Physic at the above University, the 23 of Aug.
M.DCC.LXXX.

University and King's College, Aberdeen. 1893. The arms are those of various families of Freeman in England and Ireland, though the crest is usually shown holding or charged with a lozenge.

ANDW. STIRLING

Crest and motto on a ribbon, with background of clouds and a sunburst. F.28199. (F.28200 is the same printed on brown tinted paper). The crest, a blackamoor's head, and motto GANG FORWARD are those of various families, notably of Keir, Garden, etc. in Perthshire and Stirlingshire and claiming descent from Thosaldus Viscomes de Striveling (Stirling), named in a charter of King David I, 1147. Incorporation of clouds and the rays of the sun suggest a date in the years around 1830, as does the white on black inscription.

DUMBARTON LIBRARY No.

Pictorial. Dumbarton Rock and Castle with the bridge over the River Leven, which joins the Clyde at the town; the three conical buildings were kilns at the crown-glass works (1777–1807) run by the Dixon family. NIF. Dumbarton has an ancient history. St Patrick is said to have been born there, and carried to Ireland by raiders. There has been some kind of fortress on the 250 foot high rock for over 1500 years, and "Dun Breatann" was probably the centre of the kingdom of Strathclyde from the fifth century until 1018. William Wallace was imprisoned briefly in the Castle after his capture by the English in 1305; and Mary, Queen of Scots sailed from there after a short stay, and it remained a centre for her supporters. With the development of shipbuilding, Dumbarton flourished in the nineteenth century, and "Cutty Sark" was built at its yard in 1869. The Dumbarton Library was founded in 1797, and the bookplate was engraved probably very soon after. It is a charming depiction of aspects of the old town, and its motto roughly translates, "Reading with delight and in like manner instructing (or urging on)". Incidentally, though not shown on the ex-libris, the royal burgh's arms (Azure an elephant passant argent tusked or bearing on his back a tower proper) were first recorded at Lyon Office 1672–7, but their first use was on the burgh's seal in 1357. The bookplate was later adapted for use at the town's Mechanics Institution Library.

Sir James Gordon Bart. of Letterfoury

Pictorial-armorial. The arms are Gordon, as Huntly with no mark of cadency and with Sutherland in pretence and impaling Glendonwyn. They rest against a tree in the foreground, supported by a pleasant but rather lackadaisical young man skimpily wreathed around the loins, and Letterfourie (the usual spelling) House – completed by Robert Adam in 1773 – is in the background; the motto on the ribbon of the badge of a baronet of Nova Scotia is in the foreground, claiming the attention of a rather charming whippet. NIF. James Gordon, 8th of Letterfourie (1779–1843), co. Banff, was son of Alexander Gordon of the same (1715–97), the 7th Laird, who took part in the Jacobite rising of 1745 and fought at Culloden. He subsequently settled in Madeira, where he joined his elder brother James as a partner in the wine trade, and succeeded him in 1791. Gordon married in 1801 Mary, first daughter and coheir of William Glendonwyn of that Ilk and of Parton, co. Kirkcudbright, and she bore him four sons and three daughters. In 1804 he was served heir male and heir of line general to his fourth great-grandfather, Sir James Gordon, 1st of Letterfourie. Two years later he was served heir male general to his cousin, Sir William Gordon, 6th Bart. of Gordonstoun, and he therefore assumed the baronetcy, although he did not formally submit his claim. Sir James

was succeeded by his eldest son, William, and his widow died in 1845. This bookplate, like the above, is an instance of precise depictions which preserve a record of places as they were long ago; for Letterfourie House has not changed significantly, though the two wings have been given another storey. The view is of what is now the back, and the front elevation is much grander.

FALKIRK CARRON & GRAHAMSTON Library No. MECHANICS INSTITUTION No.

Engraved label. Sgd: Jno smith Inv.l & sculp. This is naive graving, and its elusive maker is not to be confused with the stipple engraver John Smith of Edinburgh, fl.1800–37. Other engravers who signed ex-libris for Mechanics Institutes include Stevenson, of Aberdeen, who produced an armorial for the library there, and J. Sutherland, of the same, whose armorial for it was probably engraved years earlier. The market town of Falkirk, Stirlingshire, which includes Grahamston and, a mile north, the Carron Ironworks, was and is a place of much industry. The Mechanics' Institute movement developed from George Birkbeck's lectures to Glasgow mechanics on Saturday evenings from 1800. Within the next four years he often had audiences of 700 or more, and by 1849 there were said to be at least 400 such Institutes. See *The Bookplate Society Newsletter*, September 1990, pp. 30–34 for a note about some of them which used ex-libris. It is interesting that the Dumbarton Library ex-libris, already shown, was also adapted to serve its "MECHANIC INSTITUTION LIBRARY". A print examined was numbered 457, so its holdings were not insignificant.

Sir James Gordon Bart. of Letterfoury

John Johnson Collection, Bodleian Library, Oxford

No. Belongs to the Caledonian Literary SOCIETY. Instd. Feby. 22d. 1805

Pictorial showing Hope with her anchor leaning on an oval supported by books within a landscape. Sgd: J. Gordon Sculp., another elusive engraver, but one clearly inspired by Thomas Bewick. This society was in Aberdeen, and two catalogues survive in Aberdeen University Library, the earlier dated 1814.

No. J. KELLY. TIN-PLATE WORKER. Edinburgh

Wood-engraved landscape, the subject of which is Edinburgh from the north. In the centre can be clearly seen the tower of St Giles' Cathedral with, behind, Salisbury Crags and Arthur's Seat, whilst at far right is the Castle. One imagines that the oblongs below the old town are the recent terraces of the new town. Sgd: J. Ross, PRINTER. All the wording is letterpress. The earnest little homily below, entitled "KNOWLEDGE IS POWER", perhaps derives from Francis Bacon's *Religious Meditations. Of Heresies.* NIF. v.8560. George and James Ross, printers in Edinburgh, were at Horse Wynd Donovan's 1804, James was at Horse Wynd in 1805 and West Bow the following year, and George was at No. 5 1806–11, moving to No. 14 1812–17. They published amongst other things children's books, and Ross's Juvenile Library in collaboration with James

Lumsden of Glasgow. The engraving was obviously a "universal" one insofar as it was available in the printing shop for use as and when requested by clients.

T. KIDD & CO's. Circulating Library No…. No.4 High School Wynd, EDINBURGH

Oval festoon engraved label. NIF. Liverpool Public Library Collection.

W. REID'S NEW CIRCULATING LIBRARY 40. Shore Opposite the New Draw Bridge. Leith. STATIONERY & NAUTICAL WAREHOUSE

Decorative engraved label incorporating, aptly for a port, a sailing ship. Sgd: Chas Thomson Sc. 42 High St. Edinr. NIF. Liverpool Public Library and Pincott Colls. Charles Thomson, fl. 1800–30, was sometime at Cross, Edinburgh as well as the address given above. He engraved plans of Scottish towns, 1823–27, and made many bookplates.

Inst.ᵈ Feb.ᶦ 22.ᵈ 1805.   J. Gordon Sculp

J. ROSS. PRINTER.

"KNOWLEDGE IS POWER."

Remember, Reader, thy Creator intended thee in this stage of thine existence, not for speculation, but for action: the cultivation, therefore, of thine intellectual powers ought ever to have a particular respect to the enlargement of thy sphere of usefulness in society. If thou forgettest this in thy literary pursuits, thou art only fulfilling a lust of the mind—thy knowledge will deepen thy condemnation, and give additional emphasis to the reproaches of thine own heart.

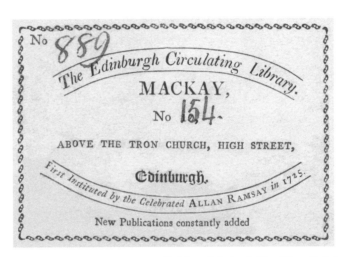

**The Edinburgh Circulating Library. MACKAY
No. [154] ABOVE THE TRON CHURCH,
HIGH STREET, Edinburgh. First Instituted by
the Celebrated ALLAN RAMSAY in 1725.
New Publications constantly added**

Printed label with rectangular ornament border. NIF.
Bodleian John Johnson Collection. The reference to
Ramsay is historically very interesting, for Allan Ramsay
(1686–1758), the Scottish poet, in 1726 set up shop in the
Luckenbooths, Edinburgh, where he became a bookseller
and founded the first Scottish circulating library. The latter
did not meet with universal approval, and (1728) the Rev.
Robert Wodrow, in his *Analecta*, Vol. 3, p. 515, commented
that Ramsay obtained from London "all the profane and
obscene books and playes" and lent them "for twopence a
night or some such rate" to "young boys, servant weemen
of the better sort, and gentlemen, and vice and obscenity

dreadfully propagated". The magistrates went to check on
him, but he had notice of their coming and hid the worst. It
became a great library, and Sir Walter Scott observed that he
later read in it as a young man with great avidity. In 1757
John and Margaret Vair took the business over, Mrs. Vair
later continuing it as a widow, and she sold it to James
Sibbald in 1780. It was in decline by 1799, when James's
brother William attempted to revive it under the management of John Stevenson. At Stevenson's death it was sold
to Alexander Mackay, who did well with it, but at his
retirement in 1832 he liquidated the entire stock at public
auction. A large proportion became part of William
Wilson's bookshop at 44 George Street, which lasted until
1851. Over the years its favour with the literati was impressive, as was its longevity. There is another Mackay printed
book label (Liverpool and John Johnson) which reads:
MACKAY, SUCCESSOR TO GRAY, AT THE OLD EXTENSIVE
CIRCULATING LIBRARY, A LITTLE ABOVE THE TRON

CHURCH, HIGH STREET, EDINBURGH. No." William Gray's circulating library was at the front of the Exchange in Edinburgh by 1772 – so that adds another strand to the story.

There were, of course, too many other Scottish circulating libraries to detail here, but it may be helpful to list several which used ex-libris. Alexander Angus & Son, of Castlegate, Aberdeen used a beautiful large Chippendale engraved label (Tanner Collection); Alexander Brown, Broad Street, Aberdeen, used a pictorial plate (ex Julian Marshall Collection); J. Burnett of Aberdeen's pictorial engraved label is F.34282; a print of Archibald Coulbrough of Glasgow's printed label is in the Henderson Smith Collection; McLachlan & Chalmers of Dumfries's Chippendale pictorial is F.34352; and a printed label used by Nicholl of Dundee is – like a number of other ex-libris there is no space for here – in the Tanner Collection.

Robt. Anderson Dunse

Pictorial with the inscription in a wreath of thistle supported by three cherubs; a female classical figure at lower left crowns a girl with laurel, and there are clouds as background. NIF. The place indicated is Duns, the capital of Berwickshire, which was often spelt Dunse until recently. In view of the composition of this plate one cannot but suspect that Anderson was a schoolmaster and that this was the ex-libris for his school library. It has the same character as eighteenth century premium or prize bookplates, though they include space for the name of the pupil awarded to be added in manuscript. See Lee, *Premium or Prize Ex-libris*, 2001, where several illustrations show the crowning of scholars.

THE AYR SHIRE Circulating Library for GENTLEMEN & LADYS. By James Meuros Kilmarnock

Chippendale pictorial engraved label, the upper compartment depicting a cherub holding open a book inscribed "No. Vol." accompanied on the right by either a decrepit cherub or a bald-headed man who hasn't bothered to dress; inscription in the compartment below. Sgd: H Gavin Sculp. Edinr. NIF. There is a print in the Turnbull Collection at the Fitzwilliam Museum, Cambridge. This composition may also have served the purpose of a trade card. Hector Gavin (1738–1814), son of David Gavin, bookkeeper in Holland, worked at addresses in Parliament Close from 1774, and was still there 1809–12 with his son Hector in partnership.

The Fitzwilliam Museum, Cambridge

They then seem, until Hector senior's death a couple of years later, to have worked independently. Hector junior (1784–1874) was at 150 High Street from 1813, but then had several workshops. In 1856, in his retirement, he went to live with a married daughter.

ILDEPH: KENNEDY

German armorial-pictorial of a monumental character, with globes at the top of columns at left and right, Ildephonsus Kennedy (1721–1804) was a Scotsman who had migrated to Germany by 1759, for from then on he belonged to and held office in several learned societies. An ecclesiastic in the Scots Cloister at Regensburg, Bavaria, from 1773, he was an Electoral Ecclesiastical Counsellor and Censor of Books for Bavaria. The arms depicted suggest that he was of the Kennedy family of which the Marquess of Ailsa is the head, but he is unidentifiable in available pedigrees, and Ildephonsus may well have been the name he adopted in religion. His bookplate was etched for him by his friend Count Johann Caspar Aloys Larosée, and the weird and idiosyncratic Latin inscription testifies to his being a most agreeable friend. Larosée made a bookplate for himself in 1769, and this one is probably roughly contemporaneous in date. See the *Ex-Libris Journal*, Vol. 7, 1897, p. 30.

H. McCorquodale

Spade shield single coat armorial-pictorial, the arms resting against a tree trunk, rose and thistle decorating at the sides. NIF. The arms are as McCorquodale of that Ilk and Phantillans, Argyll, registered at Lyon Office 1672–67. Perhaps Hugh McCorquodale (d. 1848) merchant in Liverpool, the son of Archibald McCorquodale, and believed to be great-grandson of Duncan McCorquodale of Phantillans who had Charter of that barony in 1629. From Hugh descend the paper manufacturing McCorquodales.

Ardoch (Moray)

Quartered and impaled armorial (Moray quartering Strathearn impaling Stirling quartering Sinclair) in the Jacobean manner. F.2164. Colonel Charles Moray (1746–1810), 15th Laird of Abercairny, Perthshire, who succeeded his elder brother Alexander in 1784, was the third son of James Moray, 13th of Abercairny (1705–77) and of Lady Christian Montgomery, daughter of the 9th

Ardoch.

NAPIER

Earl of Eglinton. He was in direct male line descent from Sir William Moray who was killed at the Battle of Stirling in 1289. Moray married the eldest daughter and heir of Sir William Stirling of Ardoch, Dunbartonshire, 2nd Bart., thus bringing the Ardoch estate to her husband.

NAPIER

Quarterly armorial (Napier quartering Scott), baron's coronet above, within a ribbon bearing the mottoes, badge of a baronet of Nova Scotia depending. F.21548. Francis, 10th Baron Napier (1819–98), was educated at Harvard and Glasgow and Edinburgh Universities. He was Envoy Extraordinary and Minister Plenipotentiary to the United States 1857–9, to the Netherlands 1859–61, Ambassador to Russia 1861–4, to Prussia 1864–6, Governor of Madras 1866–72, and acting Viceroy of India 1872. Created Baron Ettrick of Ettrick in the peerage of the United Kingdom in 1872, he became a Knight of the Thistle and a Privy Councillor. He married in 1845 Anne Jane Charlotte (d. 1911), only daughter of Robert Manners Lockwood. She bore him four sons, the eldest of whom, William John George, succeeded him.

JOHN KEIR ESQ.

Gothic-style single coat armorial-pictorial. Sgd: RICHD. SMIRKE DEL 1811. ABM RAIMBACH SCULPT. F.16864. Richard Smirke (1778–1815) studied at the Royal Academy Schools and became an antiquarian draftsman. He was

RICHᴰ. SMIRKE DEL. · 1811 · ABRᴹ. RAIMBACH SCULPTᵀ.

much employed by the Society of Antiquaries. Abraham Raimbach (1776–1843), born in London the son of a Swiss who had settled in Britain, engraved after Reynolds and Wilkie, etc. John Keir (1768–1851), of Westfield, Edinburgh, was the fifth but second surviving son of James Keir of Kinmounth, Perthshire, and of Margaret Orme. He was twice married but was predeceased by his children. Keir used several other ex-libris, two of them unsigned versions of this one.

Macdonald of Ulva

Allegorical armorial (quarterly coat of Macdonald), showing Minerva seated on a rock, holding a spear and supporting the oval bearing the armorial on her knee; a rocky scene with an owl in the foreground. Sgd: Engd. by Kirkwood & Sons. F.19140. Reginald (otherwise Ronald) Macdonald, 2nd of Ulva, an island adjacent to the Isle of Mull, fourth son of Colin Macdonald, 2nd of Boisdale in Skye and of Ulva (which he purchased), and of Isabella, his second wife, daughter of Robert Campbell. James Kirkwood (d. 1827) and his son Robert (1774–1818) and grandson, also Robert, were engravers in Edinburgh, at various addresses including Parliament Square and 11 South St Andrew Street. James married Christian Anderson at Perth in 1772, and his son Robert married Janet, daughter of John Mitchell, at Broughton in 1796. Fincham, and others, were unable to differentiate the works by the above and those of a contemporary Kirkwood in Dublin. Who did which is discernible from the biographical details of owners, and the output of both businesses was sizeable.

Macdonald of Ulva

Phoebe Dunbar

Single coat armorial, crest and motto above, inscription below, within a picture frame. NIF. A virtually identical composition, reading Margaret Dunbar (F.9261) is of different engraving, and the print in the Lee Collection is cut round the image. The arms are a differenced version of Dunbar of Hillhead, recorded at Lyon Office 1672–7. Perhaps Phoebe, youngest daughter of Duncan Dunbar, merchant in London who married Phoebe Bailey, and sister and heir by entail of John Dunbar of Sea Park, Forres, Moray. She married in 1848 Edward Dunbar of Glen Rothes, Moray (b. 1818), who assumed by authority of the Court of Session the additional surname of Dunbar, i.e. became Edward Dunbar Dunbar. They had five children and Phoebe died in 1899. Margaret was probably an elder sister of Phoebe.

Earl of Fife.

Earl of Fife

Armorial (Fife quartering Duff, with an escutcheon of pretence for Sinclair), with supporters and a baron's coronet, all on an ermine-lined mantle, and with an earl's coronet above. F.9197. James Duff (1729–1809), 2nd Earl of Fife in the peerage of Ireland, succeeded his father, William, the 1st Earl, in 1763. MP for Banffshire 1754–84, and for Morayshire 1784–90, he built a harbour, for which he obtained a charter, in the Burgh of Macduff on the Moray Firth. In 1790 he was created Baron of Fife in the peerage of Great Britain, and he was Lord Lieutenant of Co. Banff 1795–1809. In 1759 he married Lady Dorothea Sinclair, only daughter of Alexander, 9th Earl of Caithness, from whom he was separated *c*.1771, and died childless.

Charles Lawson. No.

Crest within a wreath of thistle. Sgd: Wm. Mitchell. Sct. Edinr. NIF. Mitchell's career remains elusive, though he worked in Edinburgh. He did, however, engrave a pictorial ex-libris for John Campbell near Bonnington Bridge (NIF), which occurs printed on white, green and yellow paper, and is probably *c*.1830–40. Bonnington Bridge is in the outlying parts of Edinburgh. What is especially interesting compositionally about the Lawson plate, apart from its elegance and ambition, is its harking back to the Chippendale style, by then so long outmoded, especially in the motto ribbon and its decorative endings. The crest and motto were recorded at Lyon Office in 1868 for Lawson of Halheriot – later Robertson Lawson – when Lord Provost of Edinburgh. He was of the Edinburgh grain merchant family.

Anonymous (Baron Elphinstone)

Single coat armorial in a simple Jacobean-type cartouche, with baron's coronet, the motto on a ribbon aside the arms. NIF. Most probably the bookplate of John, 13th Lord Elphinstone (1807–60), who succeeded his father in 1813 when aged six. A professional soldier, he became captain in the Royal Horse Guards in 1832. In 1835 he was made Governor of Madras, privy councillor, and knight of the Royal Hanoverian Guelphic Order. A lord in waiting to Queen Victoria 1847–52, he was then appointed Governor of Madras. During his term of office the Indian Mutiny took place, when "his resolution, ability and tact was of the highest order", and he received the thanks of parliament. In 1859 he was created a peer of the United Kingdom as Baron Elphinstone of Elphinstone. On his death, unmarried, his British peerage became extinct and he was succeeded in his Scottish honour by his cousin, John Elphinstone Fleming.

Anonymous (Maitland Heriot)

Wood engraved armorial (Maitland of Ramornie impaling Agnew) with supporters, etc. NIF. Armorials in that medium have always been uncommon, but this and the ex-libris below show how effective lettering white on black can be. Frederick Lewis Maitland Heriot of Ramornie, Fife (1818–81), was the eldest son of James Maitland Heriot of the same (1774–1848) who in 1792 assumed the surname and arms of Heriot in lieu of his patronymic of Maitland following his successful claim, and being served heir to that estate under entail made by Captain William Heriot in 1771. He was great-grandson of Charles, 6th Earl of Lauderdale (1688–1774). Ramornie had been the property of the Heriot family since 1512 by grant of James VI, though it had been leased to them since 1481.

SIR HUGH SEYMOUR BLANE Bart.

Single coat woodcut armorial. F.2796. Sir Hugh (1795–1869), 2nd Bart. of Blanefield, Ayrshire, was the second but eldest surviving son of Sir Gilbert Blane, MD, physician in ordinary to George III, who was created a baronet in 1812. His armorial bookplate (F.2795) shows Gardner in impalement, for he married in 1786 Elizabeth, daughter of Abraham Gardner. Sir Hugh Seymour Blane, who was a lieutenant-colonel in the army, married in 1832 Eliza, daughter of John Armit, Esq., of Dublin. His grandfather, Gilbert (d. 1771) was an Indian "nabob".

The Rt. Honble. Lord Gray

Single coat eared shield armorial with coronet, supporters, etc., within a frame of leaves and tendrils. Both the crests depicted were used by the family at different times. Sgd: Lizars sc. F.12577–8, the latter printed on pale pink paper. He had other bookplates (F.12579–82), which likewise occur on tinted papers. For a note on Lizars see p. 18. John, 16th Lord Gray (1798–1867) was the only son of Sir Francis, 15th Lord, and his wife Mary Anne, daughter of Lt.-Col. James Johnston. He succeeded his father in 1842. A representative peer for Scotland 1847–67, he had no children by his marriage in 1833 to Mary Anne, daughter of Colonel Charles Philip Ainslie of the 4th Dragoons, and on his death he was succeeded by his sister, the Hon. Madelina Gray (1799–1869).

William G. Jamieson Aberdeen

Crest and motto. NIF. The crest and motto are given in Burke's *General Armory* for this surname; and the arms with crest and motto were first recorded at Lyon Office in 1856 for Jamieson of Croy, Dumbartonshire.

Fettes College

A bee volant in pale proper and above it the motto INDUSTRIA, from the crest and motto of Fettes, of Wamphray, co. Dumfries, Bart. Sir William Fettes (1750–1836) was born in Edinburgh, the son of William Fettes, who was a merchant there. He became a wine and tea merchant, underwriter, and contractor for military stores, etc., and acquired great wealth. Fettes retired from business in 1800, the year he became Lord Provost of Edinburgh, and four years later he was created a baronet. He founded Fettes College for orphans or the offspring of needy innocent unfortunates. The trust fund was allowed to accrue, building began in 1864, and the College opened in 1870 on land which had been part of Sir William's Comely Bank estate in the Inverleith area of Edinburgh. Its alumni have included the Prime Minister Tony Blair.

Dr. D. Butter

Eared shield single coat armorial within a frame, the upper and lower part of Greek key pattern, the upright ones incorporating the rod and serpent of Aesculapius. Sgd: D. Butter. EDINR. 1820 J. & G. Menzies. F.4682–4, on white, yellow and red papers, but it also occurs on green. John and George Menzies, engravers in Edinburgh, were at Clamshell Turnpike 1805–6, and thereafter at various addresses until 1842. J. Menzies engraved a plan of Perth, 1809, and with G. Menzies engraved numerous maps of Scottish counties, railways, etc., between 1816 and 1831. Dr. D. Butter, who as you see designed this plate for himself in 1820, was Inspector-General of Hospitals in Bengal. The arms are those recorded at Lyon Office in 1672 for Butter of Gormack, and used by various branches of the family, doubtless descendants, including, until re-matriculation with appropriate marks of cadency in 1907, Butter of Faskally and Pitlochry, Perthshire.

Anonymous (John Patersone)

Single coat armorial of very antiquated, rather Tudoresque, style, with motto FAR AND SURE and a hand grasping a golf club as crest, all within a border in the form of a damaged architectural moulding. NIF, and unrecorded by Fincham. The cartouche below is here blank, but it also occurs with the name in manuscript. Underneath, engraved as if on a rectangular parchment, is an inscription in dog-Latin and "I hate no person", an anagram of the owner's name. The inscription roughly translates: "Victor in the game which is peculiar to the Scots After thrice three ancestors were crowned with laurels Paterson(e) lifted from the ground into the sky This ball which bore so many winners home".

A.Deuchar Fecit

cum victorludo ſcotis qui propriuseſſet
ter tres victores poſt redimitus avos
patersonus humo tunc educebatinaltum
hanc quœ victores tottulit unadomium

I hate no person

Sgd: A. Deuchar fecit (see below). Few bookplates of this period, probably *c.*1800–1810, were engendered by a sense of fun, and Patersone's pride in his golfing prowess is made very clear.

ALEXR. DEUCHAR SEAL ENGRAVER. EDINBURGH

Sunburst with space at centre for the number of a book, within a circlet bearing the inscription, "EDINBURGH" below on what would normally have been the motto ribbon. Above is a tiny version of the Royal Arms as borne 1801–37 (it is too indistinct to be more precise about its date). NIF. Alexander Deuchar, seal engraver in Edinburgh, married there Christian Mitchell on 31 July 1787. The coloured printings of his bookplate deserve comment. Prince Albert (see p. 98) used book labels in various colours, as did Sir William Stirling Maxwell (see p. 103), but Deuchar had done the same markedly earlier. There are four prints of this plate in the Lee Collection. The one numbered "52" is in brown, and has manuscript shelf-marks. So too has "205" printed in orange. Number "345" is in black and on thicker paper. "457" is on a green tinted paper and, though apparently from the same copper as the others, is a second state, for within the garter bearing the inscription is added "TO HIS MAJESTY", no doubt George IV. See the following.

David Deuchar Seal Engraver to His Royal Highness Geo: Prince of Wales EDINBURGH

Quarterly spade shield armorial on an inscribed plinth; it is supported by cherubs, and incorporates crest, Prince of Wales' feathers and a modest trophy of arms. v.8377. Though of typical bookplate size, its inscription and appearance suggest that it may also have served as a trade card. F.8538 is a second state, with totally different arms and crest: Or a wolf's head erased a chief ?azure. *Burke's General Armory* gives for Deuchar of Edinburgh: Argent a sword in pale azure hilt and pommel or quartering gules a boar's head couped or, and these occur on other of the Deuchar ex-libris. David Deuchar (1745–1808), son of Alexander, sometime lapidary in Edinburgh, married secondly on 15 September 1776 Christian Robertson. He practised in Edinburgh and in 1803 published three volumes of *Etchings from Masters of the Dutch and Flemish Schools*, with some original designs by himself. An etcher of some skill, he discovered Raeburn's bent towards portrait painting, gave him some instruction and introduced him to David Martin. There is a portrait of him in the Scottish National Portrait Gallery. See Redgrave's *A Dictionary of Artists of the English School*. His eldest son, Alexander, who married Jane Turnbull, was an Edinburgh engraver who died *c.*1845, and one cannot but wonder whether the bookplate detailed above was not perhaps his rather than that of the Alexander cited there, who eludes the pedigree in Alex. J. Warden's *Angus & Forfarshire its land & people*, 1882, which is sizeable and quite useful but eschews dates and other than bare bones of a surprisingly complex tale.

Mary Hamilton Nisbet Ferguson

This and the following are nineteenth century so-called "die-sinker" armorials. The Ferguson is unusual in showing two achievements side by side: Ferguson with Nisbet quartering Hamilton in pretence; and Nisbet quartering Hamilton on a lozenge with supporters. F.10387. Mary Hamilton Nisbet of Belhaven and Dirlton, Mrs. Ferguson of Raith, was the only child of William Hamilton Nisbet (b. 1747) of Belhaven and Dirlton, and of Mary his wife, daughter of Lord Robert Manners. She married firstly Thomas Bruce, 7th Earl of Elgin, which marriage was dissolved in 1808, and secondly Robert Ferguson (d. 1840) of Raith, Fife, MP. On her death she was succeeded in the Belhaven and Dirlton estates by her daughter of the first marriage, Lady Mary Bruce, wife of Robert Dundas.

Robert Brown. Underwood Park, Paisley

Single coat armorial. NIF. Robert Brown (b. 1810) of Underwood Park, Paisley, Renfrewshire, was brought up at Low Capilly Farm, Neilston, and worked as a reporter and sub-manager of *The Glasgow Chronicle* before being appointed Town Chamberlain of Paisley in 1834. He

Mary Hamilton Nisbet Ferguson

resigned in 1845 and set up business as an accountant and later as a sharebroker. In 1850 he founded Ferguslie Fireclay Works on the outskirts of Paisley, and in 1854 he became a member of Paisley Town Council and a junior magistrate. By 1855 he was a senior magistrate, and was 1855–59 Provost of Paisley. In 1874 he owned 34 acres of land at Underwood, adjacent to the works, with a gross annual value of £1,264.15. Subsequently he published several books on the town including a two-volume *History of Paisley*, 1886. Brown died post 1893. The arms are those recorded at Lyon Office 1680–87 for Thomas Brown of Eastfield, Bailie of Edinburgh (c.f. Stodart, *The Browns of Fordell*).

General Sir Thos. Makdougall Brisbane, Bart. G.C.B - G.C.H &c. &c. &c. OF Brisbane and Makerstoun

Armorial: quartered coat of Brisbane quartering Makdougall with baronet's badge at mid point, insignia of GCB and GCH dependent, supporters and three crests, Brisbane, Makdougall and Hay of Alderston. F.3742. Sgd: Lizars, sc., for a note on whom see p.18. An earlier crest plate for Brisbane has already been illustrated, and it probably belonged to Sir Thomas's father. Sir Thomas Makdougall Brisbane (1773–1860) succeeded his father in 1812. He joined the army in 1789 and had a distinguished

General Sir Thos. Makdougall Brisbane Bart
G.C.B - G.C.H. &c. &c. &c.
OF
Brisbane and Makerstoun

military career, serving in Flanders, the West Indies, Spain and North America. Governor of New South Wales 1821–25, he was also a noted astronomer and catalogued 7,385 stars whilst in Australia. Brisbane is named after him. F.3743 is an anonymous proof of his bookplate.

SIR JOHN DICK LAUDER. BART. FOUNTAIN HALL

Armorial: Lauder quartering Dick with Cumin in pretence, with supporters, two crests, and three mottoes, the badge of a baronet of Nova Scotia pendant beneath the shield. F.17685. Sir John Dick Lauder of Fountainhall and Grange, 8th Bart. (1813–67), succeeded his father in 1848. He served for 12 years in the East India Company's Bengal Army, and in 1845 married Lady Anne Dalrymple, daughter of the 9th Earl of Stair. The escutcheon of pretence should not appear, since it rightly belongs to the arms of Sir John's father, Sir Thomas (1784–1848) who married in 1808 Charles Anne (d.1864), only child and heir of George Cummin of Relugas, Moray.

PRINCE ALBERT'S LIBRARY

Label for the spines of books, the inscription in a garter with coronet above. NIF. It occurs in two sizes, the larger 38mm high. Printed in gold on different coloured papers (russet, pink or white, yellow, blue, pale green, bright green, red, brown and orange) to indicate classification. The central circle was for the volume number. Probably the

work of Andrew Gibb, the Aberdeen printer. See Lee, *British Royal Bookplates*, 1992, No.4, p.23. Prince Albert (1819–61) of Saxe-Coburg & Gotha, married Queen Victoria in 1841. Enlightened and artistic, he designed their Scottish home, Balmoral, and organised the 1851 Great Exhibition.

L (Princess Louise, Marchioness of Lorne, later Duchess of Argyll)

Entwined L's bound by a marquess's coronet, royal coronet above. Unsigned. NIF. HRH Princess Louise (1848–1939), the fourth daughter of Queen Victoria and Prince Albert (above), married in 1871 John Douglas Sutherland Campbell, Marquess of Lorne and later 9th Duke of Argyll, sometime Governor-General of Canada. There were no children of the marriage. A fine sculptress, the Princess made their home at Kensington Palace a centre for artists, and she was a firm supporter of education for women; but they also lived at Roseneath (now demolished). See *British Royal Bookplates*, 1992, No.117, p.137.

CHARLES & MARY TREVELYAN

Pictorial-armorial. Sgd: WBS 1857–8, and thus the work of William Bell Scott (1811–90), the painter, illustrator, critic and poet. This is one of four Trevelyan bookplates, all of similar design but with the inscriptions and arms altered as appropriate; but this last one was produced after Bell Scott's death and occurs in two varieties, the earlier having a label

SIR JOHN DICK LAUDER, BART.
FOUNTAIN HALL.

for cadency of an eldest son. See p. 20 and *The Bookplate Society Journal* for March 1986, where there is an article on Bell Scott's ex-libris and his place in bookplate history. Wallington Hall is seen in the distance through the arch, with the arms of Trevelyan impaling Bell above. Charles Philips Trevelyan (1870–1958), 3rd Bart. of Wallington and son of Sir George Otto Trevelyan, 2nd Bart., was an MP and President of the Board of Education He married in 1904 Mary Katharine, daughter of Sir Hugh Bell, 2nd Bart.

PARISH OF WICK CARNEGIE PUBLIC LIBRARY 1898

Pictorial-armorial sgd: G. WhittAKER 1898. Wick has been a Burgh of Barony from about 1400 and was created a Royal Burgh by James VI in 1589. The bookplate's central feature is taken from the second seal of the Burgh, adopted in 1832, showing St Fergus standing in a boat on the sea, rowed by two men, holding a crozier in his left hand, his right raised in benediction. Gwladys Whittaker lived at Leamington, Warwickshire. She exhibited in 1901 twelve ex-libris she had designed and etched, including this one.

(Primrose, Earl of Rosebery)

Anonymous quarterly coat armorial, the arms within the Garter. Archibald Phillip Primrose (1847–1928), 5th Earl of Roseberry, was the elder son of Archibald, Lord Dalmeny (1809–51) and Lady Catherine Lucy Wilhelmina Stanhope, daughter of 4th Earl Stanhope. He succeeded his grandfather, Archibald, the 4th Earl, in 1868. Lord Lieutenant of Lothian and Linlithgow, and a JP for Buckinghamshire, he had a remarkable political career. Under-Secretary in the Home Department 1881–83, he became Lord Privy Seal and 1st Commissioner of Works, 1885, Secretary of State for Foreign Affairs 1886 and 1892–4, and was Prime Minister, 1894–5. Special Ambassador to Austria, 1910, he was created Earl of Midlothian, Viscount Mentmore and Baron Epsom in 1911. This bookplate cannot be earlier than 1892 when he became a knight of the Garter. One of the few Scottish peers to be KG as well as a knight of the Thistle, he was furthermore awarded the Royal Victorian Chain. Honours indeed!

Natural History Society of Glasgow PRESENTED BY HIS SISTER & BROTHERS with 150 other Vols. to the Natural History Society of Glasgow, as a Memorial of PROFESSOR THOMAS KING President of the Society 1893-96, October, 1896

Armorial (Glasgow's arms) label, in brown. Founded in 1851 by nine "gentlemen interested in the pursuit of natural science", similar organisations merged with it: Glasgow Naturalists Society in 1866, Glasgow Society of Field Naturalists, 1871, Glasgow Practical Naturalists Society, c.1890, and Glasgow Eastern Botanical Society in 1898. The Andersonian Naturalists' Society and the Microscopical Society of Glasgow were amalgamated in 1931 in what is now Glasgow Natural History Society. Encouraging the

study of natural history, chiefly in the west of Scotland, it has a council of *c.*20, a full programme of annual events, and its library is in the Graham Kerr building at Glasgow University. Thomas King (1834–96) was born at Lochwinnoch, Renfrewshire, third son of James King. A frail child, he became an English teacher, but due to poor health went in 1864 to Chile. There he taught, and collected botanical specimens, some new to science. Back in Scotland he studied botany, in 1889 became Professor of Botany in Anderson's College Medical School and next year the same at Glasgow Veterinary College. He joined the Natural History Society in 1878. See *Transactions of the Natural History Society of Glasgow*, Vol. 5, NS, 1900, pp. 1–17, for his life.

Royal Philosophical Society of Glasgow

Pictorial: a classical female figure with petasus, etc., perhaps representing Mother Earth, the inscription in an oval ribbon. NIF. It began in 1802 when 22 citizens met in the Prince of Wales' Tavern and formed a committee to plan a Society "for the improvements of the Arts and Sciences" in the city. Needing a select library of scientific books, the next year new publications were bought in London, and soon afterwards 71 journals came by post. In 1812 a librarian was added to the council. A problem was premises, and from 1831 meetings were held in the Andersonian Institute where the library was housed. The Society moved in 1868 to the new Corporation Galleries in Sauchiehall Street. In 1880 the Society joined the Institute of Engineers and Shipbuilders in erecting a new building in Bath Street, again moving in 1906, but the building was sold in 1961, and the 5,000+ volume library was dispersed. Lecture halls were then rented, and since 1994 meetings are held at Strathclyde University. Its distinguished honorary members have included Lord Kelvin, Professor Pavlov, Sir Arthur Evans, Sir Ernest Rutherford, and Albert Einstein.

EX LIBRIS Glasgow Archaeological Society

Gothic seal armorial printed in embossed red with the city arms, St Mungo featuring sizeably as crest. NIF. Founded in 1856 for the professional, political and mercantile elite of mid-nineteenth century Glasgow passionate about their city. They were fascinated by the Old Town which was rapidly disappearing before their eyes. In their early days they were closely associated with the Old Glasgow Club and the Royal Philosophical Society (above), sharing lectures and members. The society's publications, field

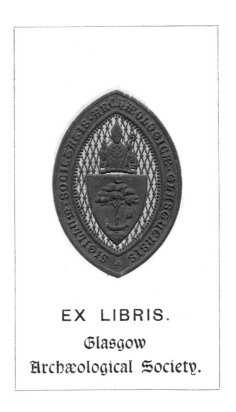

EX LIBRIS.
Glasgow
Archæological Society.

visits and other activities are accompanied by the annual Dalrymple Lectures on aspects of European archaeology, made possible by D. G. Dalrymple's considerable bequest in 1907. Its library was sold about five years ago. Some of its books bore a fancy ex-libris made for an early twentieth century office bearer, inscribed "Alexander Galloway, Foreign Secretary, Glasgow Archaeological Society".

Ex libris bibliothecae Naesmyth de Posso Baronetti

Circular seal armorial (Naesmyth quartering Baird of Posso, with large oval badge of a baronet of Nova Scotia depending. NIF. No specific baronet is named but it was probably commissioned by Sir John Murray Naesmyth of Posso and Dawyck, Peeblesshire, 4th Bart. (1803–76). It seems likely that the intention was use by him and his successors, but the Franks Catalogue lists three other seal armorials (F.21520–22), attributing them to his son Sir James, 5th Bart. (1827–96). The estate of Posso came to the family (originally spelt Nasmith) through the heiress Elizabeth Baird who married Michael Naesmyth in the mid-sixteenth century, this being confirmed by a grant of Mary Queen of Scots in 1554 of "half the lands of Posso with the whole mansion house and tower, garden and orchard", along with other lands. An amusing legend explains the origin of the surname. An ancestor, on the

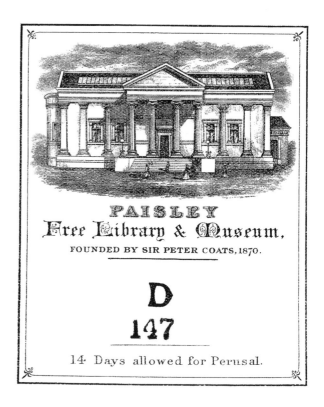

eve of battle, was required to repair the armour of King Alexander III, in which task he was far from successful, though he fought well in the battle. The king knighted him, remarking that he was "na smith but a brave gentleman". John Murray Naesmyth was a noted garden designer, both at Dawyck and elsewhere, and rebuilt Dawyck in the Gothic style. He married twice, firstly in 1826 Mary, daughter of Sir John Marjoribanks, Bart. She died in 1836, and he married secondly the Hon. Eleanor Powys, daughter of Thomas, 2nd Baron Lilford. Though unsigned, this bookplate was clearly the work of Hardman Powell, of Birmingham, founded by John Hardman (1767–1844). His son and partner, John, became in 1838 partner to Augustus Welby Northmore Pugin (1811–52), and developed a vast and widespread business. See *The Bookplate Journal* for March 1990, pp. 8–9.

PAISLEY Free Library & Museum FOUNDED BY SIR PETER COATS, 1870

Pictorial: the facade of the building, with figures in the foreground. Engraved probably on steel, but unsigned. F.33945. Sir Peter Coats (1808–90), one of the ten sons of James Coats (1774–1858), a founder of the thread industry in

Paisley, was of Auchendrane, Ayrshire. With his brother James he founded J. & P. Coats, thread manufacturers at the Ferguslie works in Paisley. He was knighted in 1869. The family were notable philanthropists and benefactors to the town. Thomas Coats gave it the Fountain Gardens in 1863 and the observatory situated on Oakshaw Hill in 1882. Sir Peter gave – as the bookplate evidences – its Free Library and Museum. His gift included many valuable books, including Audubon's *Birds of America*, which is probably the only one in the country in its original binding. He married in 1832 Gloriana, daughter of Daniel Mackenzie of Sandbank, Argyll, and they had five sons and three daughters. She died 1877. In 1881 Sir Peter and Thomas were entertained at a civic banquet and presented with their portraits painted by Sir Daniel Macnee, PRSA. The Gothic-style Thomas Coats Memorial Church was opened in 1894. The Library and Museum still exists; it was the first public library opened in Scotland; and it is housed in the building depicted, which was designed by John Honeyman.

(Sir William Stirling Maxwell, 9th Bart.)

Anonymous "subject" bookplate (see below). Sir William (1818–78), the nephew of Sir John Maxwell, 8th Bart., assumed the surname Maxwell after his patronymic. He married firstly at Paris in 1865 Anne Maria (d. 1874), third daughter of David, 8th Earl of Leven, and secondly in 1877 Caroline, daughter of Thomas Sheridan and widow of the Hon. George Chapple Norton. Vice-Lieutenant and MP for Perthshire, he also became Lord Rector of Edinburgh University. Sir William was unique in the history of British ex-libris, for not only did he design many himself and commission other artists but he loved having them printed on variously coloured papers and in ink of different colours. F.20104–20235 were all for his own use, but there were in total more than 132, as in this instance. This was one of a number, on different coloured papers for diverse subjects, for use in his libraries at Nether Pollock and Keir, and this particular Keir one was for "PROVERBS", but there were others for such as "EMBLEMS" and "A N A" &c. (whatever that may mean). One of the Nether Pollock plates was for "ARTS OF DESIGN". A bookplate for his son and successor follows (see p.124).

BIBLIOTHECA ABBATIAE S. BENEDICTI FORT AVGVSTVS

Seal armorial depicting St Benedict, with thistles in the surrounding ornament. Unsigned NIF. An armorial (F.33799), incorporating mitre and crosier, and with a rectangular border, could well have been the work of the same designer but is likewise anonymous. The Benedictine Abbey of Fort Augustus was founded in 1878 by Simon, 15th Lord Lovat and other Catholic noblemen. The school, built "to provide a liberal education for 100 sons of Catholic gentlemen", flourished for over a hundred years. The library was dispersed in 1999, following the disestablishment of the Abbey in December 1998, its most valuable books being deposited in the National Library of Scotland, Edinburgh. The print illustrated was accompanied by a printed label, within a linear rectangular border, reading: "LITTERARUM EXTRANEARUM Section ... Shelf ...".

LADY HELENA MARIOTA CARNEGIE

Single coat lozenge armorial on a feather background, inscription around. Designed by John R. Sutherland in 1919, but presumably engraved by someone else. Lady Helena (1865–1943) was the fifth daughter of James, 9th Earl of Southesk (1827–1905) to whom the honours forfeit by his ancestor John, the 5th Earl, as a result of his involvement in the Jacobite rising of 1715, were restored in 1885. Her mother was his second wife, Lady Susan Mary Murray (m.1860), daughter of the 6th Earl of Dunmore.

Charles Edwin & Janet Stein Haig

Armorial (Haig impaling Haig quartering Veitch) surmounted by the Haig rock crest and with the famous motto, which refers to Thomas the Rhymer's saying about the family, printed below. Dated 1882 aside the shield, it was designed by Harry Soane. F.13215. Harry Soane (1844–1927) was apprenticed to Thomas Moring and then took over his business in Green Street, Leicester Square, moving to 36 Hanway Street c.1890. Upwards of 600 ex-libris are attributable to him. Charles Edwin Haig (1849–1917) of Pen-ithon, Radnor and Orchardwood, Berkshire, was a barrister-at-law of Inner Temple and a JP for Radnor. He married in 1871 his cousin Janet Stein Haig, second daughter of John Haig of Cameron Bridge, Fife, and of Rachel, daughter and co-heir of Hugh Veitch of Stewartfield. Haig was the fifth great-grandson of James Haig, 17th Laird of Bemersyde, who sold that estate to his brother in 1610.

Faculty of Actuaries in Scotland Incorporated by Royal Charter 1868

Seal-style armorial-pictorial. The Faculty had its origins as part of the Institute of Actuaries in London, and held its meetings there. Its first headquarters in Edinburgh, from 1856, were in St Andrews Square, but it has moved more than once and is now at 40 Thistle Street. From 1869 to 1904 they used a circular seal, uncomfortably similar to the Royal Arms of Scotland. The bookplate and second seal, shown here, was in use 1904 to 1950. The Royal Arms and Imperial crown feature with thistles below the circular cosmic depiction, with the motto which translates "Faithful to the end". In 1950 the Faculty was granted arms by Lyon office, and these appear on the ex-libris which has been used ever since – of similar shape and dimensions to the previous one. How one wishes, though, that the 1904 composition had been signed, for it is markedly well engraved. See A.R.Davidson, *The Faculty of Actuaries in Scotland 1856–1956*, Edinburgh, 1956.

"Tyde what may betyde
There'll aye be Haigs in Bemersyde."
Thomas the Rhymer. c. 1290.

ALEXANDER B. McGRIGOR

Circular seal-type single armorial. Unsigned. NIF. Alexander Bennett McGrigor (1827–91), 3rd Laird of Cairnoch, Stirlingshire, was the elder son of Alexander McGrigor 2nd of Cairnoch (1796–1853), a JP and solicitor in Glasgow, and descended from Malcolm McGrigor (1733–93), merchant in Glasgow. The arms shown are those of MacGregor of MacGregor. In 1892 A.B. McGrigor, the only surviving son, recorded arms at Lyon Office: Argent a sword azure in bend dexter surmounting a fir tree eradicated proper, on a chief ermine an antique crown of the third; crest, A demi-lion gules holding in his dexter paw a pine branch of the third.

LADY ANNE DICK-LAUDER

Jacobean style lozenge armorial (Dick-Lauder impaling Dalrymple). Designed by her son, Sir Thomas Dick-Lauder (see p.110), and engraved in 1890 by Charles William Sherborn (see p.107). Lady Anne Hamilton Dalrymple (d.1919), eldest daughter of North, 9th Earl of Stair, married in 1845 Sir John Dick-Lauder, 8th Bart., of Fountainhall, Haddington.

E LIBRIS WILLELMI DALRYMPLE MACLAGAN STP EBORACENSIS ARCHIEPISCOPI

Traditional seal composition depicting a bishop – here probably Maclagan himself – flanked by the arms of the Archbishopric of York and the diocese of Lichfield, his personal arms beneath his feet. Sgd: ALLAN WYON SC. Allan Wyon (1843–1907), the medallist and seal-engraver, was the son of Benjamin Wyon, and the family held office as Chief

DOMINO ME REDDE MEO

105

Engravers of HM Seals from 1812. He learnt engraving under his brother Joseph, travelled abroad, in 1873 became partner in the family firm, and compiled *The Great Seals of England*, 1887. Fincham lists about 100 bookplates by the Wyons but there were many more. His son Allan G. Wyon continued the family tradition. The Most Rev. William Dalrymple MacLagan (1826–1910) studied law at Edinburgh University, joined the army, served in the Madras Cavalry until 1849, and retired on medical advice. He then read mathematics at Peterhouse, Cambridge (BA 1857), was ordained in 1858, and became curate of St Stephen's Marylebone. Rector of Newington 1869–75 and of St Mary Abbots, Kensington 1875–78, he was then appointed Bishop of Lichfield and chaplain in ordinary to Queen Victoria. In 1891 he became Archbishop of York, retiring in 1908. He was the fifth son of Dr David MacLagan (1785–1865), President of the Royal College of Physicians of Scotland. The arms of MacLagan were matriculated at Lyon Office for the bishop's brother, Professor Sir Andrew Douglas MacLagan, in 1876.

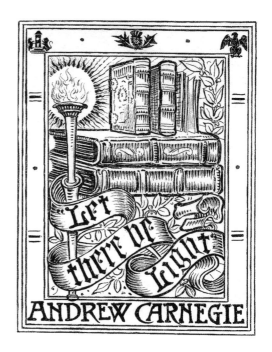

ANDREW CARNEGIE

Pictorial including books, a flaming torch and "Let there be Light", on a ribbon. Unsigned. Andrew Carnegie (1835–1919) was born at Dunfermline, taken by his parents to the USA in 1848, and aged 14 became a telegraph boy in Pittsburg. Moving to the railways and the introduction of sleeping-cars, he also invested in oil; and next concerning himself with developing the Pittsburg iron and steel industries, he built up an empire and amassed an immense fortune. After selling to the US Steel Trust in 1901 he lived at Skibo Castle in Sutherland and became a philanthropist especially keen on the establishment and equipping of libraries, and the endowment of universities. The book-plate of his wife, Louise Whitfield Carnegie, is a pictorial depicting a mother seated beside a cot in which her infant lies asleep. The border surrounding is inscribed "THE HAND THAT ROCKS THE CRADLE RULES THE WORLD". It appears to be sgd: A Dixon. The design for Carnegie's bookplate was adapted by Sir Alexander Stone (1907–98), the distinguished Scottish lawyer, banker and philanthropist, who also used another plate incorporating his portrait and the arms of Hutchesons Grammar School, the City of Glasgow and Glasgow University. Both are sgd: A.V.G.

GEORGE PATTON OF CAIRNIES

Armorial. Unsigned. F.22923. George Patton (or Paton) of Cairnies, Gleneagles, Perthshire (1803–70) was the third son of James Patton of the same, Sheriff Clerk of Perthshire, who in 1809 recorded arms at Lyon Office – Azure a fleur de lys between three crescents or within a bordure engrailed gules – which differ from those of the bookplate. An advocate at the Scottish bar and ardent Tory politician, in 1859 he became Solicitor General for Scotland, but the following year was elected MP for Bridgewater and appointed Lord Advocate. He failed next time round and was widely suspected of "gross bribery" in both elections. In 1867 appointed Lord Justice Clerk as Lord Glenalmond, it was said that, since choice of a successor to the previous holder lay with Patton as Lord Advocate, by appointing himself he sought to avoid any involvement with the bribery enquiry. In 1867 he succeeded his brother, Thomas Patton, WS, in the Cairnies estate but the following year he committed suicide. He was an enthusiastic agriculturist and forester, notable for his experiments in growing different conifers.

ARCHIBALD · HAMILTON · DUNBAR,

LATE CAPTAIN · H·M· 66ᵀᴴ REGIMENT.

1891.

ARCHIBALD HAMILTON DUNBAR LATE CAPTAIN HM 66TH REGIMENT

Armorial: Dunbar with label and Eyre quartering Houblon accollée. Sgd: CWS, and thus the work of Charles William Sherborn (1831–1912), the greatest copper engraver of bookplates of his time and author of over 400 of them. See *A Sketch of the Life and Work of Charles William Sherborn*, 1912, by his son C.D. Sherborn. The Dunbar occurs in two other states: the second with the date changed to 1897, and the third with the label removed from the arms, baronet's helm and badge, and the date 1905. Sir Archibald Hamilton Dunbar (1828–1910) of Northfield and Duffus, was firstly called 7th Bart., but later renumbered 8th, since Archibald Dunbar of Newton and Thunderton (1693–1769) should have succeeded as 4th Bart. in 1763 on the death of his cousin Sir Patrick, 3rd Bart., whose heir male he was. Sir Archibald, son of Sir Archibald by his first marriage to Keith Alicia Ramsay, daughter of George Ramsay of Barnton, was DL and a JP for the County of Elgin (Moray). In 1865 he married Isabella Mary, elder daughter of Charles Eyre of Welford Park, Berkshire who had, in 1831, assumed that surname in lieu of Houblon on succeeding to the Welford estate.

Sir William Ogilvy-Dalgleish, Bart. of Errol

Armorial (quartered coat: 1 & 4 Dalgleish, 2 & 3 Ogilvy of Boyne, with Molison in pretence), with supporters, etc. NIF. Sir William Ogilvy-Dalgleish (1832–1913) was the eldest son of Capt. James Ogilvy-Dalgleish, RN (1800–75) of Woodburne and Baltilly, Fife. Educated at Edinburgh University, he became JP for the Counties of Perth and Forfar and for the County and City of Dundee, DL for Fife and Perth, and President of Dundee Royal Infirmary, etc. In 1860 he married Elizabeth Frances, daughter and heir of Francis Molison of Errol and Murie, Perthshire. Created Baronet in 1896, he died without issue. He thrice recorded arms at Lyon Office: the first matriculation as Ogilvy-Dalgleish of Mayfield in 1883, the second as of Errol, and the third as of Mayfield in 1897. The ex-libris is therefore earlier than that year. The second and third quarterings in his arms are a rare example of a conglomerate of heraldic charges derived from various families, in this case, the lions from Ogilvy, the crescents from Edmonstone and the cross engrailed from Sinclair.

Sir William Ogilvy-Dalgleish, Bart.
of Errol.

EX LIBRIS GUI: AUG: FRASER BARONETTI 4ti.

Pictorial incorporating the lamp of knowledge and owl, putti, an urn and books. F.11294. F.11295 is the same with the signature STERN Gr A PARIS removed; but it also occurs printed on various coloured papers. Stern was the Paris firm to which fashionable people, mostly Continental, went for bookplate making in the period around the turn of the century and beyond. Sir William Augustus Fraser of Ledeclune and Moray, Inverness-shire, 4th Bart. (1828–98) was the elder son of Lt.-Col. Sir James Fraser, 3rd Bart. and his wife Charlotte Anne, daughter and heir of General Robert Crauford. JP and DL for Middlesex, MP for Barnstaple 1852–57, for Ludlow 1863, and for Kidderminster 1874–80, he lived in London, died unmarried, and was succeeded by his nephew, who became Sir Keith Fraser, 5th Bart. Sir William clearly had a penchant for ex-libris (see F.11279–95), and like some other Scotsmen favoured printings on coloured paper. The Stern ex-libris evidences this, as does his seal plate, which occurs on yellow, green and light and dark pink grounds. His ex-libris by John Leighton shown as cover illustration and on p. 33 displays the same taste (see p. 26). Though Fraser was not a member of the Ex Libris Society he was an FSA, and it was probably friendships there which drew his attention to contemporary bookplate artists and encouraged his commissioning of several of them.

EX LIBRIS JOHN MORGAN

Pictorial, the composition explained by the surrounding quotation of Psalm 127, verse 1: Except the Lord build the house: their labour is but lost that build it. There seems an anomaly, though, in the composition, as there is in the story of Jacob's ladder, for winged angels shouldn't need ladders. The one at middle left of this composition certainly

doesn't. Sgd. with CR monogram, and thus the work of Charles de Sousy Ricketts (1866–1931), who was born in Geneva and studied at the Lambeth School of Art where he met his lifelong friend Charles Shannon. They owned and edited *The Dial*, 1889–97, and ran the Vale Press 1896–1904. One of their publications was, incidentally, a volume of poems by Lord de Tabley, who as the Hon. J. Leicester Warren wrote our first major treatise on ex-libris. Ricketts was a key figure in the revival of woodcut, the medium used for this bookplate. BS.sc. indicates that the design was cut by Bernard Sleigh (1872–1954), the illustrator, decorator, and cutter on wood who was born and studied in Birmingham. John Morgan, of Rubislaw House, Aberdeen, was an architect and surveyor. A member of the Ex Libris Society, he solicited exchange of his own bookplates from 1894 or earlier, and formed a collection which after his death was sold at Sothebys in July 1908. He used a number of plates (including F.21074–6), and had a liking for architectural subjects including depiction of his own home and St Giles' Cathedral, Edinburgh.

W. R. Macdonald

Pictorial-armorial showing a mediaeval scene presumably representing labour and study. NIF. The arms, which depend from an oak tree, were recorded at Lyon Office in 1878. Sgd: GRH and dated 1886. George Roland Halkett (1855–1918) was born in Edinburgh, studied art in Paris, then returned home and produced caricatures for the press and book illustrations. Some of his bookplate

drawings are in the Viner Collection at the British Museum. The engraver W. Watson remains elusive. William Rae Macdonald (1843–1923) was born in Edinburgh, the only son of William Rae Macdonald of Mont Albion, Surinam, South America. He became an actuary, was appointed Carrick Pursuivant in 1898 and was Albany Herald from 1909 until his death. See Lee, *Some bookplates of heralds*. 2003.

Ex libris TNDL (Sir Thomas North Dick-Lauder) 1900

Landscape pictorial which appears to be engraved on wood. Sir Thomas North Dick-Lauder (1846–1919) of Fountainhall, Haddington, 9th Bart., and of Grange House, Edinburgh, was a Knight of Justice of the Order of St John of Jerusalem. He was the elder son of Sir John Dick-Lauder, 8th Bart. (1813–67) and of Lady Anne Dalrymple (q.v), second daughter of the 9th Earl of Stair. Sir Thomas died unmarried. Since he engaged in some bookplate designing it seems possible that this is an example of his own work, but cut by someone else.

NB. These last three compositions, though not comfortable bedfellows, usefully indicate the diversity of pictorial bookplate design late in the nineteenth century. Ricketts' is avant-garde, Halkett's languishes – or thrives – in love of pseudo-mediaevalism, and Dick-Lauder's reflects the survival of traditional landscape subjects which were beginning to look tired.

EX LIBRIS FRED J M CHRISTIE

Pictorial. Unsigned, but the work of Jessie M. King (1875–1949), *c.*1906. One of the luminaries of the Glasgow School of Art, who came to eminence under the tutelage of Fra. Newbery, she was a daughter of the manse. Her father was the Rev. Dr. James W. King, of New Kilpatrick Parish in Bearsden, who, after some heart-searching allowed her to study at the Glasgow School of Art. She became a book illustrator with a penchant for romantic, faery, and legendary subjects, and worked sometime in Edinburgh, London and Paris. In 1908 she married Ernest Archibald Taylor, and she lived latterly in Kirkcudbright. Her acclaim as an artist was justified, and her work has become much sought after. There is an article by Colin White on her bookplates in *The Bookplate Journal* for March 1995, and it lists 22 and records sketches which were probably never printed for use. Some were personal gifts, but others were commissions, and it is interesting that some of her ex-libris were shown at Annan's Gallery in Glasgow in 1909, at which she advertised that she charged seven guineas in black and white and ten for others with gold or silver. The coloured ones are exquisitely printed, and examples understandably tend to be the most expensive of British ex-libris made since *c.*1900.

EX LIBRIS RUTH MARY HEDDERWICK

Pictorial showing the influence of Aubrey Beardsley. Sgd: ANNIE FRENCH. The daughter of a metallurgist, Annie French (1872–1965) was born in Glasgow, trained at the Glasgow School and became a painter, etcher and illustrator. She succeeded Jessie M. King in the post of tutor in ceramic decoration. In 1914 she married George Woolliscroft Rhead (1854–1920), an etcher and stained-glass artist who also did a bit of bookplate design. Ruth Mary Hedderwick who died in recent years in her nineties came of a Glasgow family. Her grandfather, Edwin Charles Hedderwick, founded the *Glasgow Weekly Citizen* and the *Evening Citizen*. Her aunt was Jane Younger who shared a studio with Annie French in West George Street, Glasgow. Jane's bookplate reading "EX LIBRIS GEORGE MACDONALD" was probably for the poet and novelist (1824–1905), and is typically unflamboyant. The beautiful

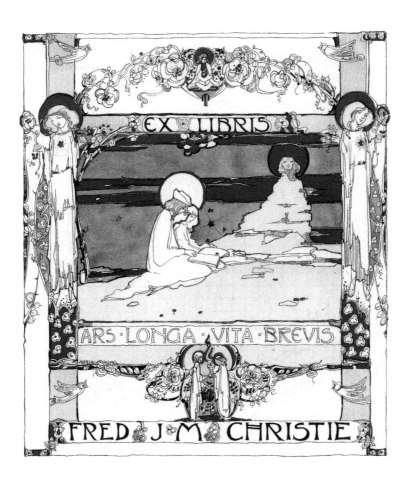

EX LIBRIS

ANNIE FRENCH.

RUTH MARY HEDDERWICK.

Ex-
Karl·Emich
Leiningen-
A·D·

Libris
Graf zu
Westerburg
1898

EX·LIBRIS

ALERE·FLAMMAM

LABORUM·DULCE·LEVAMEN

T·W·DEWAR

ex-libris she used herself, a romantic subject depicting three girls, was Annie's work. It's all rather wheels within wheels. Jane's sister was Mrs. Walter Blackie whose home, Hill House at Helensburgh, was one of the major architectural works of that now cult figure Charles Rennie Mackintosh (1868–1928), and his sister-in-law Frances Macdonald designed an unnamed pictorial ex-libris which is illustrated in *The Studio, Special Winter Number 1898–9*. There you will also find another, by Mackintosh's wife, Margaret, and a couple more by Herbert McNair. They are extremely charming and wonderfully evocative of their period and, in part, of the ambience of the Glasgow School. Original prints by those named above are, however, extremely elusive now.

Ex-Libris Karl Emich Graf zu Leiningen-Westerburg A.D.1898

Pictorial-armorial depicting St Katharine, the patron of literature, reading a book. It was printed in black, with the inscription in red, on tinted paper. Sgd: JWS. This is an interesting bookplate from a number of points of view. Its maker, Joseph W. Simpson (1879–1939) was born and educated at Carlisle and then studied art at Edinburgh. A close friend of D. Y. Cameron, who features elsewhere here, he was elected RBA in 1909, and was an illustrator, cover designer and caricaturist. Otto Schulze, the Edinburgh publisher, produced an undated monograph on his ex-libris (see p. 22). Count Karl Emich Leiningen-Westerburg (d. 1906), the author of *German Book-plates*, London, 1901, was sometime a captain of cavalry; and he became an internationally-renowned ex-libris scholar, an Hon. Vice-President of the Ex Libris Society, and a passionate collector. He favoured a plethora of personal ex-libris, and it is surely significant that he chose to commission Simpson before the artist had attained 22 years of age. It shows not only perspicacity but the liveliness of the bookplate-commissioning scene at that time and how it far exceeded national borders.

EX LIBRIS T. W. DEWAR

Pictorial etched by William Strang (1859–1921), who was born in Dumbarton, worked in shipbuilding for a year after leaving school, went to London in 1875 and studied for six years at the Slade. His chief influence was Alphonse Legros; and though his work seems to later eyes uncomfortably "dated", his portrait prints are impressive. His subjects include Rudyard Kipling, Rider Haggard, Laurence Binyon, and Thomas Hardy. He etched only two ex-libris,

listed in a manuscript catalogue by his son David only by number, but the other being for Edward Stainer. This one occurs in three states (see *British Bookplates*, 1979, No. 160, p. 110). The composition abounds with significance. One could easily read it as penitents kneeling for an episcopal blessing, but in fact the bishop, St Fillan (d. *c*.777) is proffering his crozier. The name Dewar derives from Deor or Macindeor, meaning "pilgrim" or "of the family of the Pilgrim", and they were hereditary guardians or keepers of the crozier from at least the time of Robert the Bruce. There was an agreement that villagers paid in meal annually and the possessor of the crozier was in return bound to go with the relic in search of stolen or lost goods. It was sold to the Society of Antiquaries of Scotland in 1876. Bruce was, incidentally, devoted to St Fillan, carrying into battle a reliquary said to contain his arm, and providing money towards the building of St Fillan's church.

EX LIBRIS THE SCOTTISH ARTS CLUB

Pictorial showing a rampant lion on a palette framed by thistles in silhouette. Unsigned, but designed by James Cadenhead (1858–1927), the landscape painter and illustrator, who was born in Aberdeen. He studied at the RSA School and in Paris under Duran. This ex-libris was designed in 1898. The Scottish Arts Club was founded in 1858 at 24 Rutland Square, Edinburgh, where it still flourishes.

EX LIBRIS WALTER PRESTON

Art nouveau pictorial showing a girl and tree with dwellings beyond. Sgd: W B Macdougall 1892. William Brown Macdougall (d. 1936, Loughton, Essex) was born in Glasgow, and studied at the Glasgow Academy, Julian's in Paris, and under Bouguereau, J. M. Laurens and R. Floury. He became a painter, etcher, wood engraver and illustrator, and his work from a little later than this shows the influence of Aubrey Beardsley. The composition of this bookplate provides too few clues for identification of its owner, but Macdougall also designed a bookplate reading "EX LIBRIS ARTHUR & KATE WAUGH", sgd: W.B.M. Arthur Waugh (1866–1943), the father of Evelyn, was Chairman of Chapman & Hall Ltd., and it is not unlikely that Macdougall produced illustrative work for that publishing firm. Waugh's wife, Catherine (Kate), was the second daughter of H. C. B. C. Raban.

EX LIBRIS CHARLES MARTIN HARDIE

Pictorial: a seated lady reading a book beside an urn, tree and ruins in the background. Sgd: JC monogram of James Cadenhead, for comment on whom see p. 113. Charles Martin Hardie (1858–1916) was born at East Linton, Haddingtonshire, and educated at the Free Church School there. At the School of Design Edinburgh from 1875 and the Royal Scottish Academy's Life School from 1877, he became a painter of portraits, subject pictures and landscapes, and was also a JP for the County of Fife. Hardie was a member of the Scottish Arts Club, for which Cadenhead also made the ex-libris already illustrated, and he worked at Lynedoch Studio, Edinburgh.

EX LIBRIS CISSIE ALLSOPP

Pictorial: a girl playing the piano and perhaps singing, vase of flowers and window beyond, irises framing the composition at left and right. Sgd: J. W. SIMPSON 98 on the piano lid. For a note on Simpson see p. 113. Though charmingly art nouveau, this composition offers no clues which would identify Cissie Allsopp.

ANDREW SMITH OF WHITCHESTER AND CRANSHAWS ESQR. EX LIBRIS 1897

Pictorial showing Cranshaws Castle amid trees, a dog and guns in the foreground. Sgd: J.W. Spenceley Sc. Andrew Smith (1849–1914), son of Andrew Smith of Weedingshall, Polmont, Stirlingshire, married in 1892 Ida Florence, only daughter of Walter Landale of Luttupori-Bhangulpore, Bengal. Educated by private tutors and at Neuwied, Germany, his recreations were shooting, fishing and agriculture. In addition to Whitchester and Cranshaws, both in Berwickshire, he had homes at Weston Bampfylde, Sparkford, Somerset and Weedinghall, Polmont. Interestingly, Mr Smith commissioned his bookplate from an American artist. Joseph Winfred Spenceley (1865–1908) was born in Boston, Massachussetts and worked as an engraver and etcher mostly there. A superb bookplate maker, with almost 200 plates to his credit, this was a very early work, for by 1896 he had completed only five ex-libris.

MARY E. BLAIR

Pictorial depicting Blair, near Dalry, Ayrshire, within a decorative frame including roses and thistles, books, etc., below. Sgd: INV WPB 1907, and thus commissioned from William Phillips Barrett of Messrs. J & E. Bumpus, the London booksellers. It was made by Charles Bird, RPE (fl. 1897–1907), an etcher who produced about 9% of the WPB plates. Mary Elizabeth, daughter of William Baird, of Elie, Fife, married in 1880 Col. Frederick Gordon Blair of Blair (1852–1943). She also died in 1943. Her husband's bookplate, another Bumpus commission, was engraved by J. A. C. Harrison (see Nelson, below), in 1906.

SIBELL CROMARTIE

Pictorial incorporating temples within an archaeological frame with columns of Egyptian character, and hieroglyphs, etc. Sgd: 1917 W at base of the right column. Sibell Lilian Mackenzie (1878–1962), in her own right Countess of Cromartie, was the elder daughter of Francis, the 2nd Earl, and his wife, the Hon. Lilian Janet MacDonald, daughter of 4th Lord MacDonald. A writer with a taste for mythology, she was the author of *The End of the Song*, 1904, *The Web of the Past: Sons of Milesians*, 1906, *The Days of Fire*, 1908, *Out of the Dark: Sword of the Crowns*, 1910, *The Golden Guard*, 1912, *The Decoy*, 1914, *The Temple of the Winds*, 1926, and *Heremon the Beautiful*, 1929.

THOMAS A NELSON

Pictorial showing a view of the original Nelson bookshop in the High Street, Edinburgh, with the tower of St Giles' Cathedral beyond, within a decorative wood-style frame. Sgd: INV WPB 1906, and thus commissioned as the Blair plate, above. Engraved by J. A. C. Harrison. Thomas Arthur Nelson (1878–1917), publisher and printer, of St Leonard's, Edinburgh and later of Achnacloich, Argyll, was the elder son of Thomas Nelson, of St Leonard's, founder of the publishing house of Thomas Nelson & Son, Parkside, Edinburgh. The scene depicted on the ex-libris has a charming period feel to it. John Augustus Charles Harrison (1872–1955) joined Waterlows in 1890, but before 1900 he became a free-lance engraver, engaging mostly on book-plate design. He later gained international fame for stamp and banknote designs. See Lee, *J. A. C. Harrison. Artist & Engraver*, 1983.

(Houston)

Anonymous full armorial of Houston of Johnstone. Sgd: HRW, for Hugh Robert Wallace, for comment on whom see next page. He also designed a smaller armorial, without supporters, inscribed "HOUSTON". Sgd: H.R.W. 1911. George Ludovic Houston (1846–1931), 7th Laird of Johnstone, Renfrewshire, matriculated these arms at Lyon Office in 1869. The son of William Houston (1780–1862) and nephew of Ludovic Houston, 6th Laird, whom he succeeded, he married in 1903 Anne, daughter of General Sir William Stirling, but they had no children. He was descended from George, second son of Sir Patrick Houston of that Ilk, 1st Bart. (created 1668). It is interesting that Houston "adopted" for the bookplate shown the supporters of Houston of that Ilk, evidently considering that he was entitled to them. The undifferenced arms Lyon Office allowed him in 1868 did not include supporters, presumably since it was possible, but not probable, that descendants of the senior line existed. Having emigrated to the USA in 1740, the title was not assumed after the death of the 7th Bart. in 1795. They seem to have disappeared after 1881, and were last heard of in Tallahassie, Florida.

EX LIBRIS ISOBEL M WALLACE

Pictorial art nouveau composition with panels including cockatoos and fruits, etc., inscription surrounding. Sgd: H.R.W. 1910. Isobel M. Wallace (d. 1947), the daughter of William Rae Arthur, married firstly Charles Ralph Dubs, who purchased the estate of Cloncaird, Ayrshire. Her second husband, who designed both of the bookplates shown here, Lt.-Col. Hugh Robert Wallace, DSO (1861–1924), of Busbie, had sold Cloncaird to Dubs, and so was twice of Cloncaird: before the sale, and then again after his marriage. Indeed he died there. He was male representative of the house of Wallace and descended from Malcolm Wallace of Elderslie, Renfrewshire, brother of William Wallace the patriot. His military career was distinguished. Though he had retired prior to the 1914–18 War, he then joined the Gordon Highlanders and served until 1918, being twice mentioned in dispatches and being awarded the DSO, and he was promoted to Lt.-Col. in the field.

Subsequently he became Convenor of Ayrshire County Council. He married twice, firstly in 1886 to Matilda, daughter and heiress of Archibald Campbell of Cammo, Midlothian, who bore him four children, and secondly in 1908 to Isobel McRae, as indicated above. An authority on heraldry, he designed a number of fine bookplates, principally for members of the family, Ayrshire neighbours and friends.

MORAY (Stuart)

Quarterly coat armorial. Sgd. with the monogram of Graham Johnston (see p. 26) and dated 1912. Another printing of the same is approximately half-size. Morton Gray Stuart (1855–1930), 17th Earl of Moray, was the third son of the Rev. Edmund Luttrell Stuart (1798–1869) and his wife Elizabeth, daughter of the Rev. J.L. Jackson. He succeeded his brother, Francis James, in 1909 when he died

118

without issue, and resumed the name Stuart only then, for in 1901 he had assumed the additional surname of Gray on succeeding to the estates of that family. In 1890 he married Elizabeth Douglas, daughter of Rear-Admiral George Palmer. She bore him three sons and a daughter, and two of his sons eventually succeeded to the earldom.

Ex-Libris HENRY DRUMMOND GAULD

Single coat armorial. Sgd: A. G. Law Sampson – DEL Lyon Court (see p. 22). Like Johnston, he could conjure up memorable borders for ex-libris to complement masterly heraldic depictions – and details such as the goldfinch proper as crest here are excellent. Henry Drummond Gauld (b. 1891) was the only son of Alexander Gauld of Allandale, Edinburgh, and of Mary Jane, daughter of John Dyce of Forgue, Aberdeenshire. He recorded arms at Lyon Office in 1924, and his bookplate was probably designed soon thereafter. It was Gauld's grandfather, Robert, who added the "d" to Gaul, the original surname. Our subject's seat was Kinnaird Castle, Inchture, Perthshire, and his residence Craighead, Whitehills, Banffshire.

EX LIBRIS JOHN A STEWART

Single coat etched armorial. Sgd. with John R. Sutherland's device (see p. 123) and dated 1915. John Alexander Stewart (b. 1877) was the only son of Alexander Stewart (1841–78) and his wife Euphemia, daughter of Robert Allan. His arms were recorded at Lyon Office in 1912. Stewart clearly liked ex-libris, for in all he had four by Graham Johnston and three by John R. Sutherland. Incidentally, in 1971 Leo Wyatt (see p. 132) engraved on copper an ex-libris for Henry Clark Stewart of Inchmahome, who was evidently close kin of the above. The design is based on Johnston's original 1912 painting in Lyon Register. H. C. Stewart recorded arms in 1949.

EX LIBRIS PETER JEFFREY MACKIE OF CORRAITH & GLENRISDELL

Single coat armorial (the somewhat dishevelled crows appear not unreasonably affronted at having their necks impaled by an arrow). Sgd: GJ monogram, and therefore designed by Graham Johnston. Sir Peter James Mackie (1855–1923) of Corraith, Ayrshire and Glenrisdell (normally spelt Glenreasdell) in the same shire, 1st and last Bart. (created 1920), recorded arms at Lyon Office in 1903. The eldest son of Alexander Mackie, he married in 1889

EX LIBRIS ELIZABETH C SWINTON

Lozenge armorial, a version about a third the size of the original which is signed with the GJ monogram of Graham Johnston and dated 1903 at left and right. Elizabeth, only daughter of Edward Henry Ebsworth of Llandough Castle, Glamorgan, and later of Gattonside House, Roxburghshire, married in 1895 Captain George Sitwell Campbell Swinton, Lyon King of Arms 1926–29.

A.J. MITCHELL-GILL F.S.A. Scot.. of Savock

Single coat armorial. Sgd: GJ monogram of Graham Johnston. Andrew John Mitchell-Gill (1847–1921), the only surviving son of David Gill of Blairythan and Savock, Aberdeenshire, and Margaret, daughter of Gilbert Mitchell, of Savock, assumed the additional surname of Mitchell. He married in 1894 Margaret, the second daughter of Charles S. Lindsell, of Holme, DL Bedfordshire, and she bore him three daughters. He travelled extensively in Australia, South Africa and Morocco, etc., and was an authority on genealogy and heraldry, notably of north country families. He was author of *The Houses of Moir and Byres*, 1885. His father recorded arms at Lyon Office in 1878.

Ex Libris. Thomas Douglas Wilson

Single coat armorial. Sgd: GJ monogram of Graham Johnston. Thomas Douglas Wilson (1890–1917) was the third son of Sir John Wilson of Airdrie 1st Bart., created 1906. He married in 1914 Kathleen Elize, daughter of

Jessie Lockett Abercrombie, who bore him two daughters but no son to inherit the baronetcy. The elder daughter, Jessie Isobel, married Captain George Osmond Lorne Campbell, MC, and they assumed the additional surname of Mackie.

ROBERT CLOVER BEAZLEY

Helm, crest, mantling and motto. Sgd: GJ monogram of Graham Johnston and dated 1918. Robert Clover Beazley (1850–1925), second son of James Beazley of Fern Hill, Cheshire, shipowner in Liverpool, was great-grandson of Joseph Beazley (1787–1846) who settled in Liverpool from Gosport in Hampshire. Robert's younger brother, Arthur Tetley Beazley, had a full armorial bookplate dated 1912, also by Johnston.

A. J. Mitchell-Gill, F.S.A. Scot.,
of Savock.

Ex. Libris.
Thomas Douglas Wilson.

Henry Edward Gray of Peterstone Court, Brecon, and the same year recorded arms at Lyon Office, but he was killed in action. His posthumous son, Thomas Douglas (b. 1917) eventually succeeded to the baronetcy on the death of his uncle Sir John Menzies Wilson, 3rd Bart.

(Margaret Anna Maria. Lady Campbell of Succoth) GARSCUBE

Anonymous pictorial-lozenge armorial (Campbell of Succoth impaling Borough); the scene is imaginary, for no such archway and gate existed at Garscube in Dumbartonshire. The foreground flowers are marguerites in allusion to her name, and the decoration of the wrought-iron gates includes her initials. Sgd: A Leslie 1900. Margaret Anna Maria (d. 1904), eldest daughter and coheir of Sir Edward Richard Borough. 2nd Bart. of Coolock, co. Dublin and Glenaveena, co. Meath, married in 1858 Sir George Campbell of Succoth, 4th Bart., who died without issue in 1874. Lady Campbell succeeded to all the family estates in life rent, and it was not until her death that Sir Archibald Spencer Lindsey Campbell, 5th Bart. inherited them. A. Leslie was most probably Lt.-Col. Archibald Stewart Leslie (1873–1928), 15th Laird of Kininvie &

Lesmurdie, Banffshire. He started a law career, served in the 1st World War as major Scottish Horse, became ill after service in the Dardanelles in 1915, and was invalided home. Then, attached to the War Office Staff, he was made Lt.-Col. and CMG. After his military service he was a partner in the Edinburgh law firm of Alex Morison & Co. Leslie worked sometime for the Lyon Court and etched a number of ex-libris, some of which are signed A.S. Leslie.

EX LIBRIS J. RAMSAY MACDONALD

Pictorial showing a studious owl at the prow of a sailing ship. Sgd: J.A. ADAMSON. His art career remains elusive. James Ramsay MacDonald (1866–1937) was born at Lossiemouth, the illegitimate son of a ploughman at Alves near Elgin and Anne Ramsay from Drainie nearby. He became first secretary of the Labour Party in 1900, was elected to parliament in 1906, lost his leadership in 1914 owing to his opposition to the 1st World War, but later rose to be Prime Minister in 1924 – Britain's first Labour government – and from 1929 to 1935. He it was, incidentally, who started the Cabinet Library at 10 Downing Street with a gift of three of his own books in January 1931. The library's handsome bookplate was engraved by Robert Austin that year (see *The Bookplate Journal* for March 1987).

EX LIBRIS MARY ROXBURGHE

Entwined initials within a beaded oval supported by four putti, with the Innes-Ker motto on two floating scrolls framing a ducal coronet above; below a pair of seated griffins supporting a foliage swag above the inscriptional cartouche. Sgd: N R WILKINSON 1904. The design was adapted from the printer's mark of Gabriel Giolito of Venice, *c.*1547, and the ex-libris was printed on special old paper dated 1690. Mary (d. 1937) daughter of Ogden Goelet, of New York, USA, married in 1903 Henry John Innes-Ker, 8th Duke of Roxburghe (d. 1932). The Duke bore Queen Alexandra's crown at the Coronation of Edward VII and St Edward's staff at the Coronation of George V. Sir Nevile Rodwell Wilkinson (1869–1940) was educated at Harrow, had a military career, learnt to etch under Sir Frank Short, became Ulster King-of-Arms, and took up art. His most notable work was a model palace for Titania, Queen of the Fairies, which raised over £100,000 for children's charities; but he also designed bookplates. They are recorded in *The Bookplate Journal* for March 2001, pp. 5–31.

ex libris iohannis normansell kyd

Single coat armorial. Sgd: KM monogram, and therefore the work of Keith Murray. John Normansell Kyd (1864–1931), of Pitcastle, Perthshire and Rosendael, Broughty Ferry, Angus, was the second son of David Kyd of Rosendael, of a family settled since the late seventeenth century in the parish of St Vigeans near Arbroath, Angus. He matriculated these arms at Lyon Office in 1914, with chief engrailed, his elder brother having been granted arms in 1897 and recorded them at the College of Arms the same year. Keith William Murray (1860–1922), youngest son of William Powell Murray, entered the chambers of (Sir) Alfred Scott-Gatty when York Herald. A fine artist who designed a number of ex-libris, Murray was Portcullis Pursuivant from 1913 until his death. See *Some Bookplates of Heralds*, 2003, p. 108.

Signum Theodori Radford Thomson

Single coat seal armorial. Designed by J. R. Sutherland in 1924. Theodore Radford Forrester Thomson (b. 1897), was fourth son by his second marriage to Mary Adelaide, elder daughter of Sir Henry Kimber, 1st Bart., of the Rev. Professor John Radford Thomson (1835–1918), of The Priory, Tunbridge Wells, professor at New College, London and chairman of the Society for Improving the Condition of the Working Classes. He was recognised as of Corstophine, Midlothian by Lord Lyon when he recorded arms at Lyon Office in 1958 as shown on the bookplate but with a bugle-horn sable, stringed gules in sinister chief. The family had long lived and held property in and around there, and by tradition descended from Alexander, natural son of Alexander, Earl of Mar, son of Alexander, Earl of Buchan, "The Wolf of Badenoch", younger son of King Robert II. He had further bookplates, including armorials by A. G. Law Sampson and Sutherland. John Robert Sutherland (1872–1933), a Shetlands man born at Lerwick, worked for Lyon Office and had his studio above the premises of the noted architect Sir Robert Lorimer (1864–1929) at 17 Great Stuart Street, Edinburgh. They collaborated on the Thistle Chapel in St Giles' Cathedral and the National War Memorial in Edinburgh Castle.

CHARLES GREENHILL-GARDYNE LT. COLONEL FINAVON. MCMXI EX LIBRIS

Impaled armorial (Gardyne quartering Greenhill, and Drummond), etc., the inscription in a circular surround. Lt.-Col. Charles Greenhill-Gardyne (1831–1923), 4th Laird of Finavon, Angus, was the only son of David Greenhill-Gardyne, HEICS, 3rd Laird of Finavon and of Glenforsa, Isle of Mull, who assumed the additional surname of Gardyne on inheriting the former estate on the death of his cousin James Carnegy of Craigo and Finavon. David was a celebrated big game hunter, as his son became. The collection of trophies at Finavon was well-known and was sold with the contents of the house in 1983. A couplet attributed to Thomas the Rhymer says: When Finavon Castle runs to sand The World end is near at hand" – but that refers to the original castle nearby, last inhabited in the late eighteenth century.

James Montgomery Byng WRIGHT

Quartered coat armorial (1 & 4 Wright, 2 Clark, 3 counter-quartered coat of King, Blount, Blayney and Gore – the arms recorded at Lyon Office in 1927) Sgd: A G LAW SAMPSON 1928. James Montgomery Byng Wright (c.1901–89) was the eldest son of Byng Montgomery Wright and Agnes, his first wife, eldest daughter of James Clark of Chapel House, Paisley. The Wrights were a family long resident in Inveraray as lawyers and bankers, to which burgh they gave two provosts. In 1934 Wright bought the estate of Auchinellan, Argyll, and in 1937 he again recorded arms as of that place. He had another bookplate by Law Sampson.

LT.-GENERAL SIR AYLMER HUNTER WESTON KCB DSO OF HUNTERSTON

Armorial (Hunter quartering Weston with a chief of St John), etc. Sgd: J.F. Badeley 1927. Henry John Fanshawe Badeley (1874–1951), 1st Lord Badeley, became Clerk of the Parliaments in 1934. For an account of his prolific ex-libris making see Wilson & Lee, *Bookplates by Lord Badeley*, 1993. Sir Aylmer Hunter Weston (1864–1940), 27th Laird of Hunterston, Ayrshire, was the eldest son of Lt.-Col. Gould Read Hunter Weston (formerly Weston) and of Jane, his second wife, elder daughter of Robert Hunter, 25th of Hunterston, Ayrshire. He was MP for North Ayrshire and then for Buteshire and North Ayrshire 1916–35, but for fuller details of his distinguished military career see *Who Was Who*. In 1905 he married Grace, daughter of William Strang Steel of Philiphaugh, Selkirkshire. She succeeded him in the Hunterston estate which at her death passed to his first cousin once removed.

SIR JOHN STIRLING MAXWELL

Armorial (quartered coat of Maxwell and Stirling with the badge of a baronet of Nova Scotia at mid point) within the collar of the Order of the Thistle, set against a background of tall pine trees. Sgd: W.E.C. Morgan 1931. William Evan Charles Morgan (1903–79) was a London engraver and dry-pointer of distinction, who studied at the Slade and took the 1924 Prix de Rome for engraving. His classical subjects were inspired by the sixteenth-century German engravers. Sir John Stirling Maxwell (1866–1956) of Pollok, 10th Bart., was the elder son of Sir William Stirling Maxwell of Keir, Cawder and Pollok, 9th Bart., and of Lady Anne Maria Leslie Melville, third daughter of the 8th Earl of Leven and 7th of Melville. Vice-Lieutenant of the City of Glasgow, he was also MP for Glasgow College Division 1895–1906, a trustee of the Wallace Collection and of the National Galleries of Scotland. Made a knight of the Thistle in 1929, he was also from then until 1932 chairman of the Forestry Commission – which accounts for the trees on his ex-libris. Sir John had several other bookplates, including two by Sherborn, but not the unique tally of ex-libris used by his father, who features earlier on p. 103.

PER·ARDUA

Spes·Tutissima·Coelis·

James·Montgomery·Byng·
WRIGHT

A·G·Law·Samson·1928

AQUILA NON CAPIT MUSCAS CURSUM PERFICIO

L⸍ GENERAL
SIR AYLMER HUNTER WESTON
KCB DSO
OF HUNTERSTON

J.F. Badeley 1927

AM
READY
GANG
FORWARD

SIR JOHN STIRLING MAXWELL

W. E. C. Morgan 1931

ROBERT FINNIE McEWEN ESQ.
of Marchmont and Bardrochat

Armorial (McEwen quartering arms of affection for Finnie). Sgd: WPB 1923, and thus commissioned from Messrs. J & E. Bumpus, the London booksellers, but engraved by Osmond. Robert Osmond (1874–1959) became a distinguished ex-libris maker with over 500 examples to his credit. See Lee, *Bookplates by Robert Osmond*, 1998. Robert Finnie McEwen (1861–1926) of Marchmont, Berwickshire and Bardrochat, Ayrshire, was the only son of the Rev. John McEwen (1803–66), minister of Kirkmichael, Ayrshire, and of Isabella, daughter of William Finnie. He succeeded to Bardrochat in 1874 on the death of his uncle James McEwen (1801–74) and purchased the estate of Marchmont in 1908, where he restored the magnificent eighteenth century house of the Earls of Marchmont, installing a fine organ – which he played, being a considerable musician. He was a member of the Royal College of Music 1906–26. The McEwens had been tenants of Bardrochat since the seventeenth century. Mr McEwen's son, Sir John Helias McEwen, 1st Bart. (1894–1962), politician and poet, used the same engraving for his bookplate with the inscription altered.

EX LIBRIS AVA STEWART

Pictorial: framed by trees at left and right, the eighteenth century doo'cote (dovecote) at Murdostoun Castle, Newmains, Lanarkshire. Agnes Violet Averil (Ava) (1901–75), the elder daughter of Brigadier-General Douglas Campbell Douglas, 20th Laird of Mains, Dumbartonshire, married in 1928 Captain John Christie Stewart of Murdostoun (1888–1978), son of Sir Robert King Stewart, KBE. Under the name Averil Stewart she wrote: *Scotch Broth*, 1939, *The Links of Clyde*, 1941, *My Spring and Theirs*, 1945, *Mercury in the Garden*, 1946, *Alicella: Memoirs of A.K. Stewart and Ella Christie*, 1955, and *Family Tapestry*, 1961.

EX Libris H.M. Wilson. Belchester

Pictorial: a humorous and charmingly spirited composition showing two crocodiles upstanding supporting a shield, etc. Beneath the shield there appears to be either a signature, perhaps "Robin" or a motto beginning "Robur". Hyacinthe Mary (b. 1899), the third daughter of James Hunter (1855–1924), of Medomsley, co. Durham, and of Anton's Hill and Belchester, Berwickshire, married in 1923 Major T.H. Gladstone of the Queen's Dragoon Guards, and bore him a daughter. She married secondly, in 1934, Lt.-Col. C.E. Wilson.

EX-LIBRIS LILIAS FRASER

Etched pictorial, with sundial, lilies, the Tweed and Eildon Hills in the background within a rectangular border of strawberries and their flowers. The sundial neatly corresponds, pictorially, with the motto; the aptness of the lilies is self-evident; and the scene could represent either the neighbourhood of the owner's home or a specially-loved place. The view depicted is probably the one known as "Scott's View", since it is said to have been Sir Walter's favourite. The fish in the river in the middle distance look larger than double-decker buses, but conveniently fill an unshaded space, and probably represent a sporting taste unsurprising in that part of the country. Unsigned.

MARIE LOUISE MAXWELL-SCOTT

Pictorial-armorial showing two oval shields accollé (dexter, 1 Scott of Abbotsford, 2 & 3 grand quarters counter-quartered Maxwell, Earl of Nithsdale, Maxwell, Herries, Constable and Haggerston of Haggerston, 4 Halliburton;

sinister, Logan). The shields are surrounded by belts inscribed with the mottoes of Scott and Logan and surmounted by the Logan crest flanked by thistles and lilies. Beneath the name on a central scroll is the crest of Scott with books on each side, a bust of Sir Walter Scott and the statue of The Border Reiver by Thomas Clapperton (1879–1962) at Galashiels, the additional motto "Watch well", all within a border of thistles and fleurs-de-lis. Sgd: RO 1932 J & E.B, and thus commissioned from J & E. Bumpus and engraved by Robert Osmond, mentioned on the previous page. Marie Louise St Paul de Sincay, Comtesse de Beaucaire (d. 1969), daughter of Major John A. Logan of

Youngstown, Ohio, married in 1928 as his second wife Major-General Sir Walter Joseph Constable Maxwell Scott, CB, DSO, DL (1875–1954), of Abbotsford, Roxburghshire, created a baronet in 1923.

SIR JAMES BELL BART.

Pictorial-armorial etched in 1902 by Sir David Young Cameron (1865–1945), son of a Scottish minister. He started his life in commerce whilst studying at the Glasgow School of Art, became a major topographical etcher, and his Scottish drypoints were particularly acclaimed. Hind's *The Etchings of D. Y. Cameron*, London 1924, lists 36 ex-libris he produced 1892–1914 and shows him to have been more prolific before the turn of the century. Sir James Bell (1850–1929), second son of John Bell and Helen, daughter of John Colquhoun, Midross, Luss, was educated at the Academy and High School, Glasgow. Of Mountgreenan, Kilmarnock, Ayrshire, he was JP and DL for the County and City of Glasgow, DL and JP for Lanarkshire, and twice

Lord Provost of Glasgow. He was created baronet in 1895. The composition of his bookplate is less heavy and dour than most by Cameron, and shows a two-masted ship, sails set, with the arms in a smaller cartouche above.

NAOMI MITCHISON Carradale

Naomi Mitchison (1899–1997) was the only daughter of John Scott Haldane, CH, FRS and Kathleen Trotter. In 1916 she married Gilbert Richard Mitchison (1890–1970), barrister-at-law, CBE, MP for Kettering 1945–64, who was created a life peer in 1964. Of Carradale House, Argyll, she was the author of over 70 books (novels, travel and biography), was "Mother" of a tribe in Botswana, a county councillor, social reformer, farmer and gardener, and altogether a delightful person. This pictorial bookplate nicely contrasts with the Bell alongside it, for hers shows a modest vessel and a directness, with its fish and fishing nets. She used, incidentally, another pictorial ex-libris, inscribed "NAOMI MITCHISON EX-LIBRIS" and portraying Carradale,

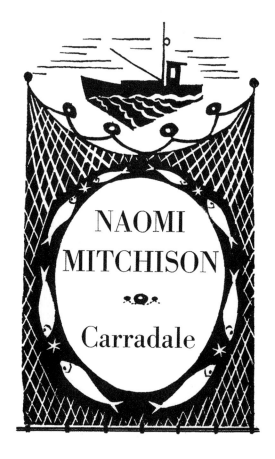

signed "Annie". It seems possible that both were gifts for they have the flavour of informality. There is a third pictorial, printed in black, blue, grey, and green. Inscribed "EX LIBRIS NAOMI MITCHISON", but unsigned, it dates from her early married days and probably depicts their house in Cheyne Walk, London.

Ex Libris The Lord Saltoun

Quarterly coat armorial (Fraser, Abernethy, Ross, and Wishart). It is signed "H P HUGGILL" in small letters bottom left, and was the work of Henry Percy Huggill (1886–1957). He studied at the Royal College of Art in London, etc., served in the 1st World War, taught in Liverpool, and was Principal of Southport College of Art 1921–30. President of the National Society for Art Education 1938–41, he exhibited paintings and engravings in print galleries in Great Britain and the colonies. Alexander Arthur Fraser (1886–1979), 20th Lord Saltoun of Abernethy, served in the 1st World War in the Gordon Highlanders, was awarded the MC, and was sometime a prisoner-of-war. He succeeded his father in 1933, and was a representative Scottish Peer 1935–63. In 1920 he married Dorothy Geraldine, the daughter of Sir Charles Glynne Earle Welby, 5th Bart. He was succeeded by his only surviving child, the Hon. Flora Marjory Fraser, his only son Alexander, Master of Saltoun, MC, having been killed in action in 1944.

HON JOHN WAYLAND LESLIE Combe Court

Pictorial quartered coat armorial (Leslie and Abernethie), a cock pheasant and a woodcock amid the mantling, the little scene below including gun, rod, landing net and trout beneath the shield, rabbits and partridges at the sides, and a frame of thistles and oak sprigs. Unsigned. The Hon. John Wayland Leslie (1909–91) was the second son of Norman, 9th Earl of Rothes. He served in the 2nd World War as a flight-lieutenant in the RAFVR, and was invalided in 1943. In 1932 he married Coral Angela, daughter of George Henry Pinckard, of Combe Court, Surrey. Another state of this bookplate is known with the address Kininvie, Banffshire.

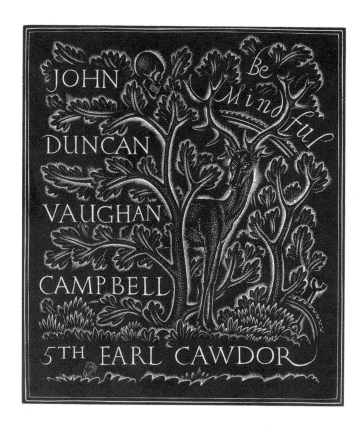

JOHN DUNCAN VAUGHAN CAMPBELL 5TH EARL CAWDOR

Pictorial showing a stag amid trees on a leafy ground. The family motto "Be mindful" is not only included but may be indicated also by the rather chastening skull at upper left. Engraved on wood by Eric Gill in 1936. The next year Gill also engraved a label for the Earl's then wife reading "Wilma Mairi Cawdor". Eric Gill (1882–1940), the artist, sculptor, engraver and book illustrator, made over 50 ex-libris and inspired wood-engraved ex-libris design for over fifty years. See Physick, *Catalogue of the engraved work of Eric Gill*, 1963, Christopher Skelton, *The Engraved Bookplates of Eric Gill 1908–1940*, and *British Bookplates*, 1979, p. 126. John Duncan Vaughan Campbell (1900–70), 5th Earl Cawdor of Castlemartin, eldest son of the 4th Earl, served in the Royal Navy in the 1st World War, and with the Cameron Highlanders in the 2nd, during which he was mentioned in despatches. He was convenor of Nairn County Council 1953–64, chairman of the joint County Councils of Moray and Nairn 1957–64, and also served as chairman of the Historic Buildings Council for Scotland and as a trustee of the National Museum of Antiquities of Scotland. In 1929 he married Wilma Mairi (d. 1982), eldest daughter of Vincent Cartwright Vickers, of Edge Grove, Aldenham, Herts., but they divorced in 1961. He married secondly, in the

slightly reduced

same year, Elizabeth Topham, daughter of John Topham Richardson, of Harps Oak, Merstham, Surrey, widow of Major Sir Alexander Penrose Gordon Cumming, 5th Bart.

EX LIBRIS Mary Russell

Architectural pictorial showing a view of Combe Manor, Newbury, seen through a lunette, with clematis, roses and morning glory festooning above, whilst on a ledge below are a lute, a print of Mellerstain, Berwickshire, home of the Earls of Haddington, and a cartouche of their armorial bearings. Lady Mary Russell (b.1934), the only daughter of the 12th Earl of Haddington, KT, MC (1894–1986) and of Sarah (d.1995), youngest daughter of George William Cook of Westmount, Montreal, Canada, married in 1954 John Adrian Bailey. After their divorce in 1965 she married David Russell. Her bookplate, signed WM del. was the work of William Maclaren, for a note on whom see pp. 29–30.

JAMES RISSIK MARSHALL Younger of Rachan

Armorial incorporating seven coats of arms. Sgd: JH (monogram), and thus by Joan Hassall, but it was drawn on scraperboard not engraved on wood, 1946. Around the family arms are, from top left: Marlborough College, Oxford University, Trinity College, Oxford, and the badge

of the Lothians and Border Horse; from top right, Edinburgh University, Faculty of Advocates, Royal Company of Archers, and the badge of the Grenadier Guards. The paternal arms were registered at Lyon Office in 1945. See the article by Leslie Hodgson, "An auto-biographical bookplate" in *The Double Tressure*, No. 20, 1996. James Rissik Marshall (1886–1959), the eldest son of H.B. Marshall, of Rachan, Peeblesshire, married in 1921 Eileen Margaret, eldest daughter of Patrick Chalmers Bruce of Baddinsgill, who bore him two sons and a daughter. Educated at Marlborough, Trinity College, Oxford, and Edinburgh University, he was called to the Scottish bar in 1912. Marshall served with the Lothians and Border Horse in France and Macedonia during the 1st World War. He was Major Commanding the same Armoured Car Co., 1926–30, Lieutenant RA (AALO) 1940–42, rising to Major in 1945. Fuller details of his career are in *Who Was Who*. The Rachan estate was sold in 1949, and he thereafter lived at Baddinsgill. His publications included *War Record of the Lothians and Border Horse*, 1920, and a chapter on the county in the nineteenth century in *History of Peeblesshire*, 1925. For a note on Joan Hassall see pp. 24 and 30.

ARCHIBALD STIRLING OF GARDEN EX LIBRIS

Circular seal-type armorial engraved on wood by Douglas Percy Bliss. Colonel Archibald Stirling (1885–1947), 9th Laird of Garden, Stirlingshire, was the only son of James

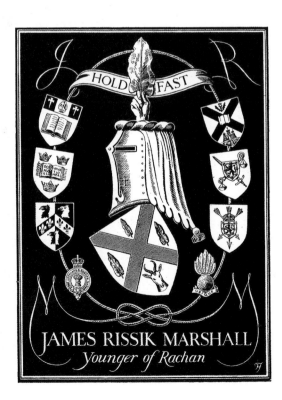

Stirling, 8th of Garden, and Anna Selena, daughter of Gartside Gartside-Tipping, of Rossferry, co. Fermanagh. He directly descended from Sir John Stirling (ante 1595–1643), 1st of Garden, which was purchased for him by his father on his marriage from Sir James Forrester of Garden. Sir John's father was Sir Archibald Stirling (d. 1630), 5th Laird of Keir and 2nd of Cawder, who descended in the direct male line from Thoraldus de Striveling named in a charter of King David I, 1147, and still alive in 1153. Douglas Percy Bliss (1900–84) was educated at George Watson's College and Edinburgh University, and studied painting at the Royal College of Art. He made *c.*30 ex-libris, and there is an article on them and him in *The Bookplate Journal* for September 1990. His son's ex-libris follows.

STIRLING OF GARDEN

Arms of Stirling accollé with Wood-Parker on a lozenge bound with a belt reading 9TH AUG. 1958; crest of Stirling and mottoes – somewhat conflicting – of both families. Unsigned, but designed by Don Pottinger. Col. Sir James Stirling, KCVO CBE (b. 1930), 10th Laird of Garden, is the only son of Col. Archibald Stirling, OBE, by Marjory his wife, daughter of Major William Stewart of Ardvorlich. He married in 1958 Fiona, eldest daughter of Douglas Alwyn Charles Wood-Parker of Keithick, Perthshire, who assumed the additional name of Wood on succeeding to the estate of Keithick in 1952 on the death of his cousin, Norah Anne Brodie-Wood of Keithick. The bookplate was commissioned as a wedding present from Colonel James Stirling's uncle, Major William Stewart of Ardvorlich, and includes the date of their marriage. John Inglis Drever Pottinger (1919–94), always known as Don, was a portrait painter, illustrator and heraldic designer. A part-time herald painter at Lyon Office, he became Unicorn Pursuivant in 1961 and Islay Herald, Lyon Clerk and Keeper of the Records in 1981. He is more widely remembered for his witty illustrations to Sir Iain Moncreiffe's *Simple Heraldry*, 1953, *Simple Custom*, 1954, and *Blood Royal*, 1956. See *The Bookplate Journal* for March 2002, pp. 50–55.

David Burnett

Calligraphic book label engraved on wood by Leo Wyatt, 1971. Wyatt also made a pictorial plate for him the following year, showing an eighteenth century gentleman reading in front of his fire. Alfred David Burnett (b. 1937) was

STIRLING
OF GARDEN

educated at George Watson's College and Edinburgh University. David, a poet and patron of the arts, was a library assistant at Glasgow University Library 1959–64 and assistant librarian at Durham University Library 1964–90; and he has published many works. Leo Wyatt (1909–81) was for many years a commercial engraver in Britain and then South Africa. Most of his numerous ex-libris were made after he returned to England and became a lecturer. Those on copper show the influence of his teacher, George Taylor Friend, and those on wood the inspiration of Reynolds Stone, below. See Lee, *Bookplates and Labels by Leo Wyatt*, The Fleece Press, Wakefield, 1988.

Barbara (Countess of) Moray

Book label, including coronet and monogram, engraved on wood by Reynolds Stone in the late 1960s. Barbara (d. 1996), the daughter of John Archibald Murray, of New York, married in 1924 Francis Douglas Stuart (d. 1943), 18th Earl of Moray. Reynolds Stone (1909–79) was a classic and prolific engraver of ex-libris on wood, and renowned more widely for his book decorations and so much else. There are checklists of his bookplates and labels in *The Private Library* for Winter 1983 and the *1998 Year Book* of the American Society of Bookplate Collectors and Designers.

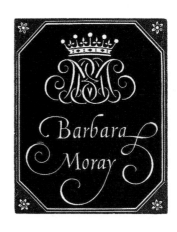

IAIN BAIN

Pictorial, engraved on wood by Richard Shirley Smith, 1980. The curious rock formation shown is called McFarquhar's Bed, and is on the Black Isle, not far from Cromarty, the home of Mr Bain's family. It was at McFarquhar's Bed that the great nineteenth-century stonemason-geologist Hugh Miller did some of his early fossiling in the old red sandstone. Miller was a Cromarty man, and his books include *My Schools & Schoolmasters*, now a minor classic. Another, *The Old Red Sandstone* proved to be a landmark in geological studies. Iain's grandfather's sailing vessel, the "Bonny Lass", was registered at Wick and operated during the 1890s and early 1900s. It is depicted close to Eilean Donan Castle, the huge tower house built by Alexander II in the thirteenth century to combat Viking invaders. Iain Stuart Bain (b. 1934), the son of James Bain, who lived at Cromarty and Kirkcudbright, was in the Seaforth Highlanders 1953–55, was Scottish champion hammer thrower 1956–57 and 1959, and then became production manager at The Bodley Head and publisher at the Tate Gallery. He is the authority on Thomas Bewick. Richard Shirley Smith (b. 1935) is a distinguished painter, his work including murals, and wood-engraver; and though he gave up engraving soon after his 50th birthday he still designs exquisite ex-libris. See *Bookplates by Richard Shirley Smith*, the Fleece Press (as above), 2006.

Thomas and Lucy Macpherson of Drumochter

Single coat armorial with baron's coronet, supporters, etc. Sgd: GM, and thus designed by Gordon Macpherson. Thomas Macpherson, 1st Baron (1886–1965), the son of James Macpherson, of Muirhead, Chryston, Lanarkshire, was educated at St George's Road School, Glasgow. He married Lucy, eldest daughter of Arthur Butcher, of

Maclean of Dunconnel

Heybridge Basin, Maldon, Essex, and she bore him one son and two daughters. Labour MP for Romford Borough 1945–50, he was Chairman of the Clan Macpherson Association 1946–52, and of the Council of Scottish Clan Societies 1952–56. Roderick Gordon Murdoch Macpherson was born in 1926 at New Westminster, British Columbia, son of the Rev. Angus Gordon Macpherson, a Presbyterian minister of highland descent. He spent his career in the investment business, but he is also a fine heraldic artist, with over 150 ex-libris to his credit. There is an article on his designs in *The Bookplate Journal* for March 1994, pp. 11–29.

Maclean of Dunconnel

Quarterly coat armorial, baronet's badge depending, with behind the shield in saltire a key, wards outwards or, and a rod gules garnished or (insignia of the Hereditary Keeper and Captain Dunconnel Castle in the Isles of the Sea). Unsigned, but designed in 1991 by Patricia Bertram. Sir FitzRoy Hew Maclean, KT CBE, 1st Bart. (1911–96)

was the only son of Charles Wilberforce Maclean (1875–1954) and descended from Lt.-Col. Alexander Maclean, 13th Laird of Ardgour, Argyll (1764–1855). Educated at Eton and King's College, Cambridge, he was MP for Lancaster 1941–59, Bute and North Ayrshire 1959–74, and Parliamentary Under-Secretary for War and Financial Secretary War Office 1954–57. Created a baronet in 1957, he was made a Knight of the Thistle in 1993. Sir FitzRoy was the author of a number of books on diverse subjects, including *Eastern Approaches*, 1949, *A Brief History of Scotland*, 1970, *Portrait of the Soviet Union*, 1988, and *Bonnie Prince Charlie*, published the same year. In 1946 he married the Hon. Veronica Nell, second daughter of 16th Lord Lovat and widow of Lt. Alan Phipps, RN. Patricia Bertram, who was born in Edinburgh, first worked in interior design, and then joined the heraldic artists at Lyon Court in 1975. Further details of her work can be found in *The Double Tressure*, 1998.

SIR JAMES FERGUSSON OF KILKERRAN. BART.

Single coat armorial, with supporters, etc. Sir James Fergusson, 8th Bart. (1904–73) was the eldest son of General Sir Charles Fergusson of Kilkerran (1865–1951) and of Lady Alice Mary Boyle, daughter of the 2nd Earl of Glasgow. A member of the Royal Commission on Historical Manuscripts, he was talks producer, BBC, 1939–40 and BBC Overseas services 1940–44, and Keeper of the Records of Scotland 1949–69. He married in 1930 Louise Frances Balfour Dugdale, only daughter of Edgar Trevelyan Stratford Dugdale. An author, his historical works include *The White Hind*, 1963, *The Curragh Incident*, 1964, *Argyll in the Forty-Five*, 1952, *Lowland Lairds*, 1955, and biographies of William Wallace and Alexander III. The Fergussons of Kilkerran, described as "among the most ancient gentry of Carrick" (Ayrshire), were by tradition descended from Fergus, Prince of Galloway (d.1161), and certainly held the Barony of Kilkerran from 1334. They have given to Scotland many distinguished legal luminaries, including Sir John Fergusson who was created baronet 1703, and Sir Adam, 3rd Bart. (1733–1813), who unsuccessfully claimed the Earldom of Glencairn, and was a notable scholar and linguist.

EOIN FLETT SCOTT OF REDLAND

Armorial. Unsigned, but designed in 1971 by Katherine Chart, herald painter at the Court of Lord Lyon 1959–67. The bookplate also occurs in full colour. His family descends from a certain Walter Scott, believed to be of the Harden family, who landed in Orkney by accident on his way to exile in Holland, and settled there at Redland. The arms were confirmed and recorded at Lyon Office in 1967.

Reverend John Charles Maule Ramsay

Armorial framed by a priest's hat and cords, encircled by the ribbon and badge of a Knight of Malta, the badge of the Scots Guards below the inscription. Sgd: K-H, and thus the work of T. Alan Keith-Hill (d.2000) of Pendeen near Penzance. A fine Scottish heraldic designer, he produced numerous bookplates and other heraldic compositions for his fellow-countrymen. Other of his ex-libris include similar scrolled ornament around names, a conceit which perhaps deserved less prolificity. John Charles Maule Ramsay (1926–98) was the fourth son of Captain Archibald Henry Maule Ramsay (1894–1955) and the Hon. Ismay

Reverend
John Charles Maule Ramsay

Preston, daughter of 14th Viscount Gormanston and widow of Lord Ninian Crichton-Stuart. Her father was great-great-grandson of William Maule Ramsay, Lord Panmure, second son of George, 8th Earl of Dalhousie. John, who served as a major in the Scots Guards, was ordained a priest in the Roman Catholic Church in 1969.

Ex Libris Charles John Burnett Esquire HM Ross Herald of Arms

Armorial. Unsigned, but designed by its owner and reproduced by thermo-lithography printed in blue. Charles John Burnett (b. 1940), the son of Charles Alexander Urquhart Burnett and his wife Agnes, nee Watt, was educated at Fraserburgh Academy, Gray's School of Art in Aberdeen, Aberdeen College of Education, and the University of Edinburgh. He married in 1967 Aileen Elizabeth, daughter of Alexander Robb McIntyre, of Portsoy, Banffshire. Since 1967 he has worked in museums, and from 1997 has been chamberlain at Duff House, Banff, but he has numerous

other responsibilities in societies and organisations, and has published books. He had an earlier bookplate of similar design prior to his appointment as Ross Herald in 1988. See *Some Bookplates of Heralds*, 2003, p. 54, for fuller details.

ELIZABETH ANN ROADS

Oval armorial. Unsigned, but designed towards the end of the 1980s by Mrs Jennifer Phillips, nee Mitchell, herald painter at the Court of Lord Lyon since 1974. Another version, made at the same time, shows her arms impaled with those of the office of Lyon Clerk and Keeper of the Records; and she also has a fine bookplate as Carrick Pursuivant by Gordon Macpherson, 1998. Elizabeth Ann Roads (b. 1951), the daughter of Lieutenant-Colonel James Bruce, MC, and his wife Mary Hope Sinclair, was educated at Lansdowne House, Edinburgh, Cambridgeshire College of Technology, and the Study Centre for Fine Art, London. She worked for Christie's 1970–74, joined the Court of

Lord Lyon in 1975, and has been Lyon Clerk and Keeper of the Records since 1986. Since 1992 Mrs Roads has been Carrick Pursuivant – the first lady in our history to be appointed a herald. See *Some Bookplates of Heralds*, 2003, p. 120. for fuller details.

Peter de Vere Beauclerk-Dewar

Quarterly coat armorial (1 & 4 Dewar of Cambuskenneth; 2 Beauclerk, Dukes of St Albans (being the Royal Arms of King Charles II with a baton for difference); 3 de Vere, Earls of Oxford), with two helms and crests, three mottoes, etc. Unsigned, but designed by Beryl Tittensor. Peter de Vere Beauclerk-Dewar (b. 1943) is the son of James Dewar, MBE, GM and Hermione de Vere, younger daughter and co-heir of Major Aubrey Nelthorpe Beauclerk (heir-in-line to the Dukedom of St Albans), recognised by Lord Lyon in 1965 in additional surname and arms of Beauclerk. He married in 1967 Sarah Ann Sweet Verge Rudder, and they

have one son and three daughters. A genealogist, he has served numerous times as Falkland Pursuivant Extraordinary, and full details of his career are in *Debrett's People of Today*. Co-author of *The House of Nell Gwyn 1670–1974*, and author of *The House of Dewar 1296–1991*, and *The Family History Record Book*, 1991, he edited *Burke's Landed Gentry*, 2001 and has contributed to many publications. The artist Beryl Mary Tittensor, nee Pickering (1918–2003) was born in Cambridge, and studied there and at Leicester College of Art and Chelsea Polytechnical College of Art. She married F.D.S. Tittensor, bore him two daughters, moved to Scotland *c*.1955 and lived first at Stirling, then Cumbernauld, and Aberlady from 1975. Though designing bookplates from *c*.1946, it was after starting work at the Lyon Court that her compositions became more formal, and at least 15 were produced during that phase of her career. She ran a village craft shop and calligraphy studio at Aberlady until 1990, when she retired from all except recreational painting.

Stewartby

Full armorial (single coat) with coronet, helm, crest, mantling and supporters. Sgd: RJLC '01, and thus engraved by Roy Cooney. Sir (Bernard Harold) Ian Halley Stewart of Stewartby (b.1935), created a Life Peer in 1992, is the only son of Professor Harold Charles Stewart of Stewartby (d.2001) and of Dorothy Irene Lowen, his first wife. He married in 1996 the Hon. Deborah Charlotte Buchan,

daughter of 3rd Baron Tweedsmuir. Educated at Haileybury and Jesus College, Cambridge, he served in the RNVR and RNR, was MP for Hitchin 1974–83 and North Herts 1983–92, and was sometime Minister of State for the Armed Forces and for Northern Ireland. A numismatist, he was author of *The Scottish Coinage*, 1955, 2nd edn 1967, and joint author of *Coinage in Tenth-century England*, 1989. The bookplate's arms are those recorded at Lyon Office in 1937 to Sir Malcolm Stewart, who was created a baronet in that year, within a bordure azure for difference, and with the label of three points gules of an eldest son, as Lord Stewartby's father was still alive when the arms were matriculated in 2001 and the supporters granted. Roy James Leonard Cooney (b.1935) trained and qualified as a copper-plate engraver and cartographer as one of the last apprentices at the Hydrographer's Department of the Royal Navy. He has engraved ex-libris since 1981. His output has been sizeable, and he is also an adept facsimile engraver.

EX LIBRIS TREVOR LEESE

Pictorial. Mr Leese, with a great interest in sailing, had a ketch at Dumbarton, and from there toured the whole of the west coast of Scotland – hence the depiction. Unsigned, but engraved on wood by Angela Lemaire (b.1944). She lived for 11 years in the Scottish highlands, moved to Edinburgh in 1984, and to the Scottish borders in 2000. An illustrator, fine-art printmaker, painter and writer, many of her works reflect her spiritual preoccupations; but she has found time to engrave *c*.15 bookplates of charming diversity. This one dates from 1999.

Index of Owners of Bookplates illustrated or mentioned

(All references are to page numbers)

Index of Artists, Engravers and Printers

(All references are to page numbers)

The Bookplate Society

For fuller information visit: www.bookplatesociety.org

An international society of collectors, bibliophiles, artists, and others dedicated to promoting bookplate study

About The Bookplate Society

Bookplates, also known as ex-libris, have since the 15th century been placed in books to declare owner-ship. Many artists, some famous such as William Hogarth, Aubrey Beardsley and John Piper, have designed bookplates, and many celebrated people (e.g. Samuel Pepys and Rudyard Kipling) have used them, but a personal bookplate has been available to anyone owning a library and wishing to place in the books a printed design as a mark of possession. You can still acquire bookplates of all ages and styles, and in a gathering of reasonable size there may be found some interesting and even scarce items.

Founded in 1972, The Bookplate Society is the direct descendant of the world's first such organisation, the Ex Libris Society, 1891–1908, and its creation and successor, the Bookplate Exchange Club. Our purpose is to encourage the production, use, collecting, and study of bookplates. We achieve this through our publications, lectures, visits to collections, members' auctions, social meetings, and exhibitions.

We focus on British Bookplates, but our membership is worldwide. Some of our members are bookplate artists and we maintain a list of British designers who are currently willing to accept commissions. Many of our subscribers are not bookplate collectors at all, but have diverse interests in the kindred fields of heraldry, genealogy, printing, the art of the book, bibliography, engraving, graphic art, and family and local history. They find the range of bookplate design, technique and history fascinating.

Membership Benefits

The annual subscription of £30 (£34 outside the UK; or $70 or €50) payable on 1 January each year gives the following benefits:

The Bookplate Journal is published in March and September each year. In 2003 *The Bookplate Journal* commenced its second series in a new, enlarged format. The substantial articles cover well-researched essays, bookplates of individuals and families, checklists of artists (contemporary and historical), collectors and collecting, notes & queries, book reviews etc.

The Bookplate Society Newsletter appears twice a year in June and December. It gives news of meetings, auction lists, membership changes, sales and wants, and items of interest not covered in *The Bookplate Journal.*

Every two years, members receive a free book. For 2006 this was *Scottish Bookplates*, and in 2008 it will be *East Anglian Bookplates* by John Blatchly. We have an ongoing plan to publish studies of the work of artists, and to cover bookplate history by styles, themes and by different areas of the British Isles.

The Society holds two bookplate study meetings each year, usually in central London. Two other meetings take the form of bookplate auctions, in which many members participate keenly by post.

Please address membership enquiries by post to the Membership Secretary, 32 Belitha Villas, London N1 1PD or by email to: members@bookplatesociety.org

Bookplate Society Publications

Some recent titles in print are shown below (prices to members in brackets). A full list appears on the Society's website. Postage is extra and will be quoted on request to: publications@bookplatesociety.org

BOOKPLATES BY EDMUND HORT NEW
Brian North Lee 98 pages, 1999. (£10) £15

SOME NORFOLK AND SUFFOLK EX-LIBRIS
John Blatchly 154 pages, 2000. (£15) £22

PREMIUM OR PRIZE EX-LIBRIS
Brian North Lee 118 pages, 2001. (£13) £20

BOOKPLATES OF GEORGE WOLFE PLANK
John Blatchly 96 pages, 2002. (£10) £16

SOME BOOKPLATES OF HERALDS
Brian North Lee 155 pages, 2003. (£14) £20

PAROCHIAL LIBRARY EX-LIBRIS
Brian North Lee 136 pages, 2004. (£10) £16

BOOKPLATES IN THE TROPHY STYLE
Paul Latcham 184 pages, 2005. (£14) £20

SCOTTISH BOOKPLATES
Brian North Lee & Ilay Campbell 144 pages, 2006. (£14) £20